Pleasing YOUR PARTNER

An Intimate Guide to Love & Sex

Dr. Gilbert Tordjman

CLB

CLB 4542.

This edition published in 1997 by CLB

Distributed in the USA by BHB International Inc.
30 Edison Drive, Wayne, New Jersey 07470

All rights reserved

Printed and bound by GRAFICOMO, S.A., SPAIN

ISBN 1 85833 711 9

A CIP Catalogue record of this book is available from the Library of Congress

Created by COPYRIGHT, PARIS FOR CLB PUBLISHING
Models: TOM HAMAK AND YVONNE HORTON
Photographer: DOMINIQUE SILBERSTEIN
Sexologue: DR GILBERT TORDJMAN
Text: LUCE DEVILLARD
French edition: FRÉDÉRIQUE CRESTIN-BILLET
Translation: CHRIS MOONEY
English language edition: CATHY MUSCAT
Designers: ANNE FLEMING AND JACQUELINE LEYMARIE
Production: NEIL RANDLES; RUTH ARTHUR
Color reproduction: ADVANCE LASER GRAPHIC ARTS (INTERNATIONAL) LTD., HONG KONG

CONTENTS

CHAPTER 1

Male and Female Sexuality

*N*o topic generates more heated debate than the question of the differences between male and female sexuality. Men and women, the experts tell us, are miles apart sexually, and if we are to believe what we overhear in bars, hair salons, and office elevators, this gap seems to be getting wider every day.

A woman's sexual nature supposedly expresses itself through her feminine wiles and charms: the lowered eyes, fluttering eyelashes, and heaving breasts of the sultry *femme fatale*, a somewhat hackneyed B-movie figure who looks her prey up and down and says in a scorching whisper, 'I want you, terribly – but don't you dare breathe a word of it to anyone.' Temptress, seductress, vixen, and vamp, she will forever bewitch the simple and the honest with her wanton ways, her heat and lust, her multiple orgasms, and immoral, insatiable desire.

And man is wolf, the skirt-chaser, the walking libido, with the perpetual hard-on who crashes back down to earth after each orgasm, his body and soul spent, barely responsive to his lover's tender but insistent urgings.

Fortunately, sexual practice has always been able to transcend these commonly-held assumptions and stereotypes, and seek new experiences, wider horizons, and paradigms.

Whether or not you believe that men and women are fundamentally different in their sexual outlook and needs, one thing is sure: it takes mutual understanding to build a fulfilling sexual relationship.

Awakening Desires

In the 1950s, teenagers developed their approach to the opposite sex primarily through fantasy. Masturbation, 'wet dreams', and sexual daydreaming prepared them for their first heterosexual relationships.

For today's teenager, however, AIDS, the recession, identity crises, the 'cocooning' trend, and society's general withdrawal into the safer world of traditional values have all helped to perpetuate the role of fantasy in sex, even though trial periods of 'living together' on a full- or part-time basis have become common.

Nevertheless, most teenagers now discover flirting and heavy petting at an earlier age than their 1950s counterparts. They also lose their virginity much earlier in life. In short, young people are no longer willing to postpone the fulfillment of their desires.

After 1968 this attitude towards sexual fulfillment transformed society and profoundly revolutionized social mores. These days, it is not so much a question of enjoying life, but of enjoying it quickly. Wars, massacres, the threat of unemployment, and changes in sexual mores – particularly regarding women – have forced us to live fast, to take pleasure wherever we find it, and to depend on no one but ourselves.

For most young girls, however, the desire to please often masks the desire to be pleased, even in this day and age. Though we may have female politicians, pilots, university professors, and bus drivers, the old axiom that 'man proposes, woman disposes' has not entirely disappeared.

At the same time, boys are bombarded with commercials, movies, and media images in which 'assertive' women call all the shots. As a result, they fantasize about Lilith (the Devil's sensual and rebellious companion, brazen in love) and have relegated outmoded Eve (created from Adam's rib) to a dusty corner of a museum.

Alas, nothing is simple: girls will always daydream of pretty ribbons and bows, and boys will continue to mold themselves after the Schwarzeneggers and Stallones of the world, persisting in the belief that 'Me Tarzan, you Jane' is an effective pickup line.

When it comes to sex, today's teenagers tend to be far more sophisticated and advanced in their sexual attitudes than their parents were at that age.

Male Erogenous Zones

Popular myth holds that, while the entire female body is an erogenous zone sensitive to all types of stimulation, males are only receptive to certain kinds of caresses on specific areas of the body. Fortunately, the truth does not conform to these beliefs.

Both men and women respond to a whole range of stimuli, but cultural taboos often prevent individuals from fully expressing themselves and their desires. Men are obviously very sensitive to oral and manual stimulation of the penis, the scrotum, and the anus and its surrounding area, but they also enjoy having their groin, buttocks, and inner thighs rubbed and stroked, as the skin is infinitely softer and more sensitive in these areas than in others.

Gently squeezing the head of the penis between the thumb and index finger will of course arouse a man and elicit a strong erection, but fingers running up and down each side of the spine will also send waves of sensual pleasure throughout the man's body, which is equally exciting.

From both an embryological and sensorial point of view, a man's sensitive nipples and aureoles have the same powers of arousal and response as a woman's, a fact that is often forgotten during a sexual encounter.

The anus and its surrounding area is not the exclusive domain of homosexuals, but a region full of nerve endings that respond when stimulated by one or several fingers. (However, do not forget that nails are sharp, and that fingers often need to be moistened with saliva or a lubricant.)

The French refer to anal kisses as 'rose petals.' This may seem somewhat surprising, but there are few things more thrilling than seeing the rings of the anus quiver at the delicate touch of an exploring tongue. Remember, to truly discover the infinite possibilities of male sexual pleasure, you must reconsider conventional ideas of what is normal and acceptable. If it feels good, do it!

The genitals are not the only male erogenous zone. The nipples, buttocks, and inner thighs are all sensitive areas, as is the back: fingers running up and down each side of the spine will send waves of sensual pleasure throughout a man's body.

Female Erogenous Zones

A *woman's entire body is an erogenous zone, even if the breasts, buttocks,* *and vagina – especially the clitoris – are infinitely more sensitive than the rest.*

Couples speak to each other through an intimate exchange of caresses and embraces. This is a learned language with a grammar and syntax all its own, which each partner must master. To become an expert in pleasure and its release requires sensitivity to all the subtleties of lovemaking – timing, rhythm, the nuances of pressure and touch, the location and hierarchy of erogenous zones.

If a woman is touched on her hand or her arm, the nape of her neck, or the small of her back, and if the touch is allowed to build from a light, furtive brush to a fuller caress, with fingertips that are pressed gently but firmly into her skin, this will communicate a message that is both exhilaratingly sexual and emotionally comforting. It says that sex is not the only goal, that a more profound intimacy is being offered, and that she is entirely desired and desirable.

Her partner can also kiss her hand or lick her palms. French writer René Fallet writes in his book, *Baroque Love:*

> *I took this hand in mine and made a woman of it, and I made love to this woman,* > *my tongue sliding, obsessed, insistent, between each finger ... and as I licked and bit* > *Else's nostrils quivered, beads of perspiration glistened on her brow. It was clear,* > *crystal clear, that my mouth had penetrated her at a level much deeper than that of* > *the open palm of her hand.*

Similarly, an erect penis can slide between a woman's buttocks, be pressed and rubbed between her breasts, or gently slid back and forth across her vagina, rubbing across the intensely sensitive ring of her vulva.

Caressing the anal opening, with or without the penetration of a finger, can also be very arousing, provided the utmost delicacy is shown. This zone, long off-limits to 'normative' sex practice, is often so charged with moral values that touching it can 'turn off' a partner and impede any pleasures its stimulation might provide.

Lovemaking is the contact of two bodies, skin rubbing skin, and the intertwining of fantasies – an exhilarating exchange of desire that calls for imagination and audaciousness, but also for intuition, sensitivity, and mutual respect.

So as to give her the most pleasure, a man should learn *which parts of the woman's body are the most sensitive.*

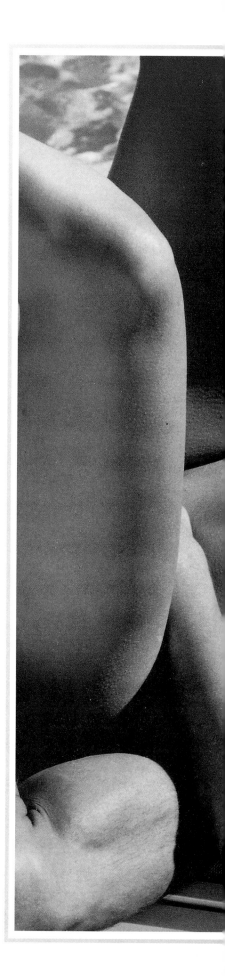

Flirting

*U*ntil the 18th century, the verb 'to flirt' meant to throw, shake or flutter. It later took on the meaning of to tease or to court. The term therefore initially conveyed the idea of something that is used quickly, then disposed of – rather like a disposable tissue. It implied that sexual contact was brief and superficial, and that the lover's aim was to get through as many partners as possible.

Today, however, the word 'flirting' tends to evoke the preliminary stage of a relationship based on love and/or sex. Flirting feeds on the glance, on kissed lips, on lightly brushing hands that grow bold, quietly and quickly slipping under a sweater to caress breasts or sliding lower to unzip a fly.

Sometimes flirting is satisfying in itself, especially when it involves verbal teasing, when erotic language accompanies discreet or more daring gestures. Flirting, as practiced today, allows girls to discover sensuality and pleasure without the commitment, real or imagined, traditionally associated with the sexual act. It also allows girls to experiment, to move from one boy to another in the knowledge that they are neither committing nor degrading themselves. Through this harmless sport, a girl can 'save' herself for her true loves, for the love that will last several weeks, months, or a lifetime. For, although sexual mores have changed, many teenagers – both male and female – still dream of a single, ideal, and lasting relationship. Perhaps this is a result of AIDS, or perhaps it reflects a more general malaise. Life in these troubled days of war, unemployment, violence, and increasing social dislocation seems so uncertain that many individuals are now turning toward more secure and comforting values.

Flirting will always be the ante-chamber of the love relationship. It stimulates not only the senses, but also the imagination, and its ultimate aim is the realization of desire.

Flirting is a way of signaling your attraction to another person,
without – at this stage – making any definite commitments to them.

The male teenager who has 'gone all the way' with a girl achieves great status in the eyes of his peer group ... he knows what life's about; he's a man now ...

*W*e have seen that flirting generally constitutes the first step in lovemaking. But 'the first sexual encounter', whether it involves just kissing and caressing or full sexual intercourse, has not become the pure formality as was predicted by a number of writers at the beginning of the 1970s.

Even though young people now talk more willingly and freely about sex than ever before, and no longer dramatize their first sexual encounters as they used to, the 'first time' remains a powerful and often distressing experience. It still constitutes a rite of passage from childhood to adulthood.

Virginity is no longer indicative of moral status in the way that it used to be. Nonetheless, for many young people, it remains a 'value' steeped in morality and taboo, and also in fear – for the girl fear of pain, and for the boy fear of not knowing what to do – which still influences young people's sexual behavior.

Today, as in the past, the first encounter between two bodies is a powerful moment. It involves personal stakes, hopes, dreams, and apprehensions, and is rarely devoid of a certain degree of anxiety. It is a momentous event that leaves indelible marks, whether conscious or subconscious, for a lifetime.

Every day, sexologists, doctors, and psychologists meet men and women with sexual problems. In some cases these problems stem not only from childhood events, but also from the way their first sexual contacts unfolded.

For example, the rape of a young girl or a furtive and hurried encounter in a car for a young boy may lay the foundations for adult frigidity, inability to reach orgasm, premature ejaculation, or impotence, to cite just a few potential problems.

The sexual revolution, therefore, has not reduced the power that the 'first time' and the 'myth of virginity' hold over both sexes. On the contrary, the power is even greater. The sexual revolution has actually individualized the problem of sex by freeing the individual of inhibitions and taboos and allowing fantasy and the quest for carnal pleasure to determine encounters. It has also inextricably linked sex to the notion of

The 'first time' remains a problematic event for most young women today: society offers few consistent guidelines about what is acceptable, as in the old days.

truth – truth of the body, the depths of genuine feeling, and the struggle for self-discovery. It is their very being that young people put at stake that first time they have sex. The experience may no longer involve the shock, trauma, pain, or obligation that so often represented the dark side of sexuality in the past, but the emotional investment is still absolute.

Another banal remark, something one might overhear in a bar or in a checkout line, but that still remains persuasive, is that boys and girls think about sex in different ways. Virginity does not have the same importance for both sexes. Desires and dreams are different across the gender line. For a boy, even if he is very much in love with a girl, the first sexual encounter will often be anticipated and then experienced in relation to the outside world and to typically masculine norms centered around the recognition of his strength and virilities. He wants to lose his virginity less for himself than for his image. The boy who sleeps with a girl has earned his stripes as a male and is acknowledged as being 'one of the guys' by his friends. He has had a hard-on; he is in the big league now. For a girl, the process of losing her virginity is a much more complex and introspective experience. The invasion of the body's intimacy has profoundly personal ramifications. Exterior sources of sexual knowledge – discussions with mother, conversations with girlfriends, and reading informative or erotic books – are few and far between. Sexual liberation is still quite recent and often contradicted by prevailing social customs. Sexual discourse, moreover, is dominated by paternalism and macho attitudes.

A young woman can withdraw into her shell with an overpowering sense that the experience cannot be truly shared. She realizes that she is a woman, not because others see her as one, but because she feels like a woman inside.

'Self-discovery,' 'revelation' – the very words often used to describe the first sexual experience show that we see it as initiating us into a different world.

In the Other's Gaze

The gaze, the first glance, the sly look, the furtive glimpse, and the penetrating stare all play an important part in the development of a romantic relationship. They allow us to gain an initial impression of the person with whom we are about to spend a few hours, a night, endless days and nights, or a lifetime.

No matter how self-controlled or implacable we want to appear, our eyes usually betray our true feelings. Our mouth can feign a smile or a pout, our jaw an exclamation or a laugh, but our eyes alone escape from this control: they darken in anger even when the mouth is smiling, and the eyes will also sparkle with joy.

We, therefore, send mixed messages: we may be laughing, but have an accusatory look in our eyes, and a friendly smile may in fact belie the serious and reproachful tone of our voice, and the eyes will either be serious or smiling.

There are countless phrases used to describe looks of attraction, interest, and love. 'Doe eyes' or 'bedroom eyes' indicate that somebody is more than simply curious or friendly. The term 'struck my eye' implies flirtation or possibly much more. 'Peeping Tom' evokes the realm of voyeurism and perverse games.

Regardless of our age or social status, we all have voyeuristic tendencies linked to infancy. Psychoanalysts refer to them as 'partial impulses.' These impulses can be satisfied in diverse ways, depending on our particular needs and preferences. For some, a mirror reflecting their lovemaking is a potent sexual stimulant. Others prefer subdued lighting shadowing the body and the face and casting a halo of charm and mystery. Still others swear by see-through garments and garishly-colored lingerie to set the tone for passion and pleasure.

The male's 'bedroom eyes' reveal that he is interested in far more than simple friendship!

The lover's gaze, whether furtive or penetrating, plays an important part in the developing romantic relationship.

How Men and Women Work

*H*uman sexuality is complex and sophisticated: we are not ruled solely by instinct or bodily needs, as are most animals. We escaped from enslavement to our hormones thousands of years ago, and are no longer tied to a libidinal calendar governed solely by the biological need to reproduce.

Male sexuality has long been considered as an instinctual, biologically-determined necessity, an innate, aggressive, and even violent need to 'come and conquer.' Hence rape, although always seen as a reprehensible act, (and which today is punishable by law in most countries), has often been described as a masculine prerogative, and seen as an expression of man's natural virility. Some people still believe that men cannot help themselves; from the playground on, many men learn that it is they who must make the first moves, who must ask and are never to be asked, who must seize, seduce, and ravish every woman who dares to stray within their grasp.

Women have traditionally been viewed as vestal virgins, as the guardians of the sacred temple of the vagina, which it is their duty to defend from all attack, on pain of suffering scorn and dishonor. Virgin worship has characterized many cultures across the ages, and the hymen – the thin vaginal membrane that only virgin women and hyenas possess – is still considered a sacred barrier to be preserved at all cost by some peoples around the world.

These commonly-held beliefs stem more from cultural and religious customs than any biological imperative. Women, just as much as men, experience the full power of desire and its demands. They, too, often like to make love for the pure, immediate, and ephemeral pleasure it provides. And men are by no means necessarily all slavering sex-starved slobs of the type portrayed in pornographic novels and movies. Like women, most men appreciate tenderness and gentle words, and rarely refuse bold advances, or will be seen to stop a forthright woman from unbuckling their belts and undoing their flies. And if a few men, the Moral Majority types, dream of deflowering their chosen ones, still more are attracted to experienced women, to women who have seen a little action and learned a few tricks of their own.

In a sexual relationship, the aspirations and values of the individuals concerned are as much at stake as their sexual needs.

Women are as
familiar with the
power of desire –
and the delights of
making love purely
for pleasure –
as men.

It is often said that
women's sexual
pleasure is diffuse,
and that the entire
female body is
erogenous. Male
sexuality is more
(but not exclusively)
penis-centered.

27

CHAPTER 2

Intercourse

A sexual relationship can often involve no more than an endless pursuit of pleasure. To come no matter what, and with no matter whom, can be all that matters. This kind of sex does not involve or require a relationship in the true sense of that word: rather, it is merely a form of mutual masturbation, with orgasm as the only goal. The *Kama Sutra* refers to this kind of sex as 'the coupling of eunuchs,' seeing it as the product of an infantile, immature sexuality whose main aim is self-satisfaction. In such relationships, the partner is merely an object of narcissistic consumption, quickly used and then discarded. On the other hand, genuine desire is fragile and capricious; to flower, it requires tenderness, passion, games, and the complicity of words and smiles. It is a way of looking at each other that conveys an intimate, private message.

The stairway to heaven should not be taken two steps at a time. It takes patience to reach the heights of pleasure. Take your time.

Seduction

'*There is a seducer for every woman. Her happiness rests in finding him.*'

(Kierkegaard, *In Vino Veritas*)

Seduction is attraction, fascination, and also bewitchment. A partner is 'taken,' enraptured, and bound in a web of desire and attraction that leaves them no respite. The seducer must 'have' and 'possess' physically and psychologically the object of his or her desire. This implies that seduction involves maneuvering and manipulation on the part of the seducer, but also surrender to passion on the part of the seduced. You will find that anything that captivates is fair game in the course of seduction – from winks to meaningful glances, and from the slightest brushing of hands (or feet under the table) to more intimate touching, once the relationship is underway.

When somebody falls under the spell of seduction, there isn't any recourse but to submit to the desires of the seducer. Think of seduction as the daughter of desire. Like her, she is unpredictable, whimsical, ready for all glories – and all degradation. She is a wild woman, living under the stars, untouched by law, oblivious to all reason.

*From changing the way we look to acting in ways
we would not usually contemplate – anything
that captivates is fair game in the course of seduction.*

Homo Erectus
Warning: Fragile,
Handle with Care

*N*o other part of the body has been the object of such veneration, flattery, conceit, and conjecture as the penis. The Hittites worshiped the penis in the form of a sacred bull. In Ancient Rome, the god Priapus protected family homes, where his effigy represented the fertility of the head of the household.

Today, it is not the sexual organ itself that is flattered and adored, but the phallus, the symbol of virility.

Contrary to preconceived ideas and fantasies, the male sexual organ is particularly susceptible to what specialists call 'flaccidity,' or – in everyday language – difficulties in 'getting it up.' Barring serious problems, an erection is usually easy to maintain, but it only takes a tiring day, an annoyance, or an irritating detail about a man's sexual partner for the whole thing to collapse.

Temporary impotency and premature ejaculation are the most frequent forms of male sexual dysfunction, and it is rare for biological reasons or disease to be the cause. Dysfunctions are most frequently caused by stressful situations, such as fatigue, unemployment, or a change in partners. Fortunately, these are benign symptoms and therefore reversible.

Yet, anxiety, fear of permanent impotence, a sense of no longer being a man, and humiliation usually accompany the inability to get an erection, which only serve to make the problem worse. The partner's full support and a visit to a doctor or counselor generally correct any problems.

Sexual dysfunction in men may simply be a response to stress, fatigue, or depression.

The Veiled Woman

*D*erived from the Latin word **velum**, *the veil is a piece of cloth used to conceal someone or something, and it plays an important role in the erotic lure of women for many men. Such men find titillating and mysterious the way a simple veil conceals the face of Muslim women, leaving only a glimpse of their eyes. In Latin countries, some men are excited by the way Roman Catholic women cover themselves with scarves or mantillas at church.*

Images of naked women, displaying all, abound in X-rated magazines, books, and movies, but many men derive much more excitement and enjoyment from seeing veiled women, with their hair covered. Throughout history, pious women have traditionally kept their hair covered, leaving men only able to fantasize about what they get up to in the privacy of their own rooms once the veil has been removed.

Modern versions of the long veils which were the trademark of 19th-century professional women's societies perhaps include hats and caps worn by policewomen and nurses. Members wore head coverings to distinguish themselves from the common populace, but, in fact, they marked the women as feminine.

So, why were women forced to conceal their hair? It is as if hair is an object of attraction and lust in itself, which perhaps is true. Looking back in time, it is clear that men (and women) have long associated hair with fertility, sexuality, and power. By cutting Samson's long locks, Delilah robbed him of his sexual power. Even today, hair symbolizes vitality. In women particularly, it is associated with their ability to have children, and to sexually capture men, to hold them hostage, and, finally, to take away their free will.

Concealment can be an erotic art, challenging the partner to fantasize about what he or she cannot see.

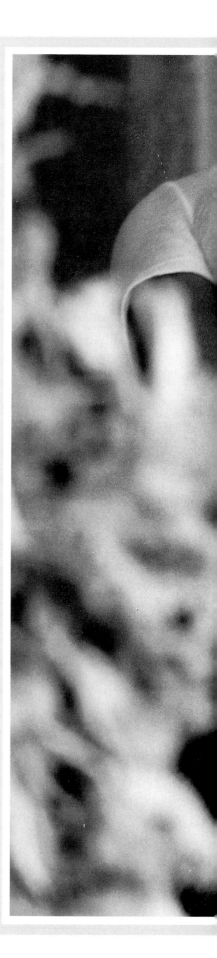

The First Touch

A first touch can be furtive or passionate. Words, looks, gentle or penetrating kisses, the brushing of hands and skin, and the discovery of scent can create an impression either of surprise or of **déjà vu** and familiarity. The initial contact is a leap into the dark, where nothing is known about the other person. It may be brutal or clumsy, but it always provides precious and essential information – which is sometimes quickly forgotten – about the other person.

Charles Maurice de Talleyrand, the 19th-century French politician and wit, once said, 'Be wary of your first impressions because they are usually right.' The first physical contact with someone engages both intellect and intuition. You will be touching somebody whom you desire but do not yet know, and you have no idea how the relationship will turn out. Your instincts will allow you to 'read' the other person and to transcend the incessant need to categorize.

The first caresses give indications about a person's basic personality, about the primal being which resists all efforts at transformation whether through psychotherapy, prayer, meditation, or social and political activism. The caresses tell your partner all about you: whether you are tender, affectionate, violent, passive, assertive, or cautious.

The way two persons touch, delicately or insistently, tells more about them than the most well-documented biographies ever could do.

With the first touch, partners make discoveries about each other's scent, skin texture, and general responsiveness.

The Kiss

The touch of skin against skin, the mingling of saliva, the discovery of a partner's scent – these are just a few of the sensual experiences united in the kiss. Kissing simultaneously expresses and stimulates sexual desire.

Though kissing is the most common prelude to lovemaking, it is not as spontaneous as might be imagined. It reveals much about your partner's culture as well as their customs. For example, though to place mouth upon mouth is an expression of love in many countries, in Slavic countries it is merely an expression of friendship; Asians forbid kissing in public; and it does not occur in the Eskimo culture where they rub noses instead. No animals are known to kiss, with the exception of certain chimpanzees, who suck on each other's lower lip before plunging into more serious sexual exploration.

Kissing has not, however, been excluded from Asian love rituals. In the Tao, feminine saliva, called 'the source of Jade,' is considered to be a source of equilibrium for men: 'The source of Jade gushes from the two orifices located under the tongue of the woman. When the man caresses the woman's tongue with his own, the liquid flows in abundance. The fluid is transparent and highly beneficial for the man.' (Wou-hien, *Libation of Three Good Work*). That poetic description of mingling saliva corresponds to what the French call a *baiser profond* and Americans call a 'French kiss.' According to the cultural anthropologist Desmond Morris, 'Human lips are unique. Of course all primates have lips, but they are not like ours, which jut out.'

Kissing simultaneously engages our five senses: the way that a mouth looks, the sense of touch, the taste and exchange of saliva, the sound of quickening breath, and the sense of smell.

There are numerous ways to kiss. The lingual kiss, in which we suck the other's tongue, is a powerfully erotic prelude that can continue during intercourse, the rhythm of the tongue matching that of the penis. Biting and sucking while kissing reminds us of the primitive origins of the mouth, whose initial function was manducation, a hardly erotic term meaning to taste, suck, chew, and speak.

Whether soft and lingering or hard and passionate, the kiss is the usual prelude to lovemaking, in the West at least.

Lingerie

'*She's more than a woman,*' *it's been said,*
The picture of perfection.
She wears chenille when she gets out of bed,
A butterfly of pure confection.
                    (Anonymous 18th-century epigram)

Lingerie, whether coquettish or erotic, can fuel the most exotic fantasies. From the fur undergarments of Sacher-Masoch – from whose name the term 'masochism' is derived – to perverse rubber, leather, or latex panties, or the red and purple transparent nylon displayed in sex store windows and favored by prostitutes, there can be no doubt that women's lingerie exerts a powerful attraction.

Embroidery, lace, and sequins provide an erotic setting for numerous real or imaginary scenes. White cotton panties are the prerogative of virgins and young girls, although some, in celebration of their newly-awakened femininity, prefer a profusion of white lace and silk.

White, black or colored underwear are all worn by mature women who will also dare to wear the lacy buttoned-up corsets that are now back in style, and are sold from mail-order catalogs, along with padded bras, bodices, and exquisitely frilly garter belts.

Never underestimate the allure of provocative blouses and deliciously revealing, frilly little snips of satin and silk in colors that are slightly *passé* – perhaps reminiscent of Hollywood movies of the 1940s, such as Rita Hayworth in *Gilda*, for example. Then there are those sumptuous, clingy, lounge dresses that Lauren Bacall or Myrna Loy always looked so glorious in. And black is dramatic and demanding, elegantly enveloping a larger woman's ample breasts and thighs.

The arrival of Lycra on the scene has certainly done nothing to reduce the seductive power of lingerie. In fact, it has widened the influence of lingerie, to the great delight of women and men in all walks of sexual life.

Whether made of satin or silk –
or even leather or rubber –
lingerie can add a great erotic
charge to lovemaking.

Undressing

'Light and short-skirted, Quickly she moves.
To be agile she wore a petticoat and a pair of flat shoes.'
(Jean de La Fontaine, PIERRETTE AND HER MILK JUG)

Clothes reveal a great deal more than they conceal. This is why, in most civilizations, there is nothing more celebrated than the nude body. For the most part, the body is hidden, leaving all to our imaginations. And because of this, many men, especially in Western societies, are actually more attracted to a sexily-dressed woman than to one who is completely naked.

The art of undressing should not be underestimated in a romantic relationship. There is nothing more disappointing than a woman who gets down to her undies in three swift gestures. Instead, undressing should be like a striptease: each garment should be languidly removed, one by one, and interspersed with kisses, caresses, and tender, erotic words.

But slowness is not necessarily a rule for seductive undressing. Sometimes, the forceful and passionate ripping-off of clothes is more suited to the heat of the moment. In these simmering circumstances, silk and lace are inappropriate for such

manhandling. But artful undressing does not only apply to women's clothes. Many men also fantasize about being undressed by a women who audaciously and skillfully undo their belts and unzip their pants.

The time taken to enjoy undressing each other will only help to heighten the pleasures to follow.

Don't rush your lovemaking:
undress each other slowly, and
allow your sense of erotic
anticipation to grow as you do so.

Foreplay

Intercourse should consist of far more than a few hasty caresses followed by penetration, however long it lasts. It should involve the hands, the mouth, and the eyes – indeed, the whole body.

One of the most common forms of foreplay is the kiss. This meeting of two mouths, tongue around tongue, is the first and foremost contact between two different skins, which may be taken further if it is enjoyable.

The caressing that follows should involve the whole body, according to each person's desires. This can center on those parts of the body that are considered erogenous – the breasts, buttocks, and genitals – but should also include the hands, hair, feet, and thighs. Sex is always best when there is something that transcends simple desire or need: a shared emotion that is so strong that it makes you think that this time, at last, you have found what you have been looking for.

Whether you choose to speak or remain silent during intercourse is unimportant. Some people chatter all the time, while others never utter a word. Anything goes, and what you do is up to you and your partner. Whispering sweet nothings can express attraction and desire just as much as saucy or obscene language, which can in turn create an exquisite sensation of transgression.

Any part of the body can become a favored erogenous zone even areas not usually thought of, if it is given the correct attention. Numerous sociocultural factors also play a part in this. In certain primitive societies accustomed to *a tergo* intercourse (see the section on positions, page 54), the back, the nape of the neck, and the shoulders are particularly sensitive to manual or oral stimulation.

In all cases, foreplay prevents sex from becoming a monotonous ritual, and perpetuates the play of attack and defense which is essential to seduction and desire.

Kisses, caresses, whispers of love: the more love and tenderness that partners show each other during sex, the better it becomes.

Caresses

*H*ands are our most sensitive instruments during a sexual encounter. Use gently stroking fingers, along with the mouth, and you will find that skin, with its warm elasticity and responsiveness to pressure, becomes second only to the genitals in its sensual receptiveness.

Caresses between men and women only become truly erotic if they are part of a genuine dialogue that is spontaneous, unconscious, and the result of years of practice – unless, of course, they are the expression of a sudden, electric telepathy between partners who have only recently met. However we look at it, the art of the caress must be part of a real exchange, in which both partners enjoy giving as much as receiving.

The caresses that come most naturally to us are centered on the breasts (for men as well as women), as well as on the anal and genital areas. This is where the hands and the mouth come into service. When thinking about caressing a partner, most people immediately think of sucking the breasts, or slipping a finger into the vagina or anus. Yet, stroking the forearm, pressing the mouth to an armpit, or touching the inner face of the thighs can also awaken hitherto unknown sensations.

As for the hands themselves, if their palms are stroked by fingertips, kissed by a half-opened mouth, caressed with hot, excited breath, then licked all over by an ardent wet tongue, they will tremble with pleasure, becoming linked through the imagination with the sexual organs.

But the hand is not the only organ of touch. Instead of the fingers, the Gutpa Indians use their fists, elbows, nails, toes, faces, and hair for their caresses. The *Kama Sutra* gives numerous examples and exercises showing how to develop the art of caressing, as do many other erotic texts and sex manuals, but it is up to each couple to invent, discover, and fantasize according to their own inner make-up and particular desires.

Use your mouth as well as your hands to caress your partner. Remember that giving is as important – and enjoyable – as receiving.

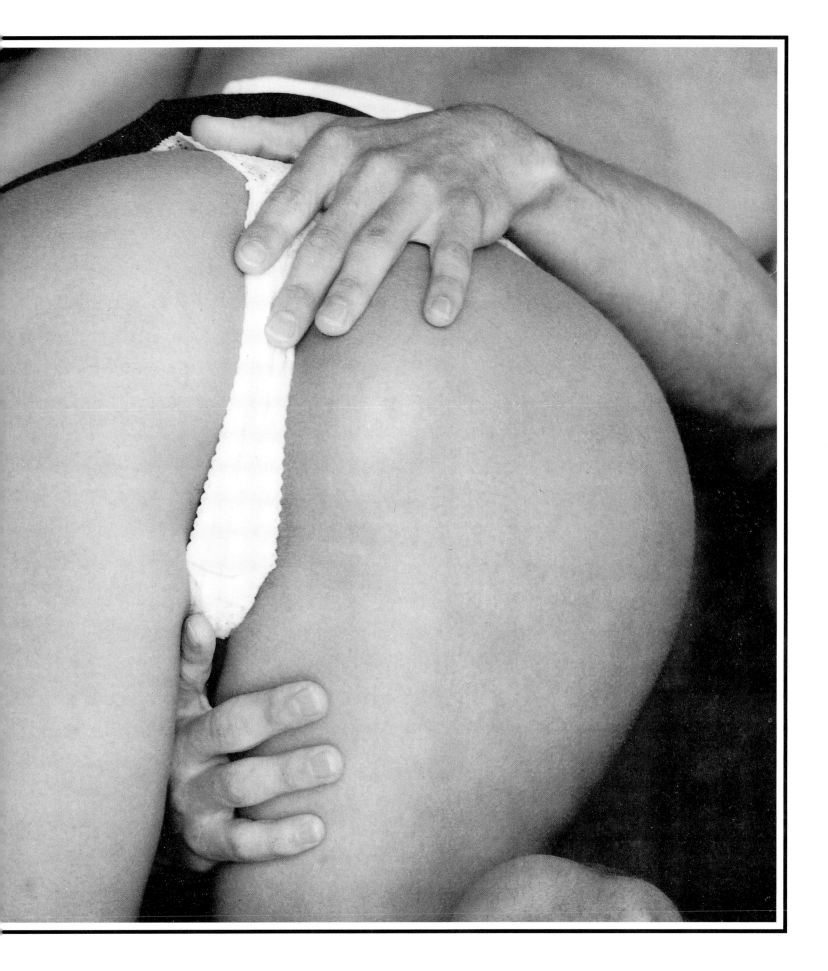

Massage

*S*troking, rubbing, pinching, pressing, tapping, sliding your fingers down the spine, tweaking the tip of a breast, kneading the buttocks – these are the simple techniques that make massage, before or after intercourse, an end in itself. Massage often awakens unknown or unaccustomed but very pleasurable sensations.

A massage requires neither costly equipment nor 'professional' skills. The hands, the face, and even the entire body in a body-to-body massage, plus some oil or talcum powder to make contact smoother, are all that is needed. To these basic ingredients, add a pinch of imagination and, above all, the desire to give pleasure, and you will be able to transform the slightest touch into a masterful caress.

There are many kinds of massage oil; some people find perfumed oils enchanting, while others find their odors intrusive and off-putting. It is best to have a good selection always on hand, or to choose them together as a couple. Other people prefer the feel of beauty cream or lotion; here, too, the perfume is important, along with the texture. Whatever the product, it should be sufficiently smooth, without being liquid, to allow easy contact between the two skin surfaces.

Begin with the soles of the feet (if the person is not too ticklish) and rub them thoroughly, as they contain numerous nerve endings. Next, massage the ankles with both hands, before moving up to the calves and then on to the thighs, which should not be kneaded too excessively.

In the beginning, you might consider avoiding the genitals and the woman's breasts, to maintain better control over the progression of pleasure. The object is not to make your partner reach orgasm in record time, but slowly to open up the whole body to sensuality. The full body-to-body massage can be an excellent preliminary to a more specific massage centered on the breasts or genitals.

A massage is a wonderful preliminary to sex. There is one golden rule to follow: use your imagination.

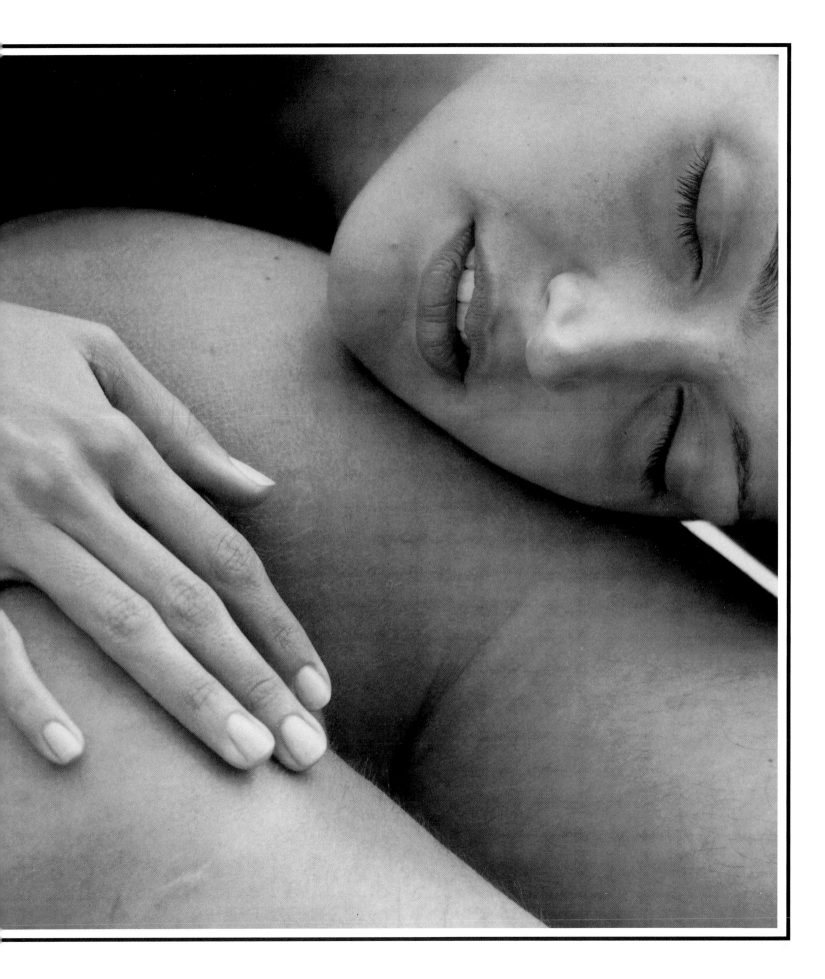

Fellatio and Cunnilingus

These are oral–genital stimulations. Fellatio involves sucking and kissing the penis, techniques that extend to the vulva, clitoris, and labia of the vagina in cunnilingus. Although a mainstay of X-rated movies and pornographic literature, such practices are avoided by people who find themselves repulsed by intimate smells or by the idea of placing their mouths on certain parts of the body considered 'shameful.'

For some men and women, sex consists of nothing more than a few quick manual caresses followed by vaginal penetration. Anything else is seen as deviating from tradition and orthodoxy. For such people, the mouth, for example, is primarily associated with the idea of nourishment. It may also be linked with kissing, but only on the cheeks or the forehead, in a friendly gesture, or on the lips of the mouth.

Many such men and women see oral sex as being 'dirty,' given the proximity of the genitalia to the anus. But the practice is only 'filthy' if one's partner is physically unclean, which is why personal hygiene is so important if a couple are fully to enjoy oral sex together. This does not mean we have to eliminate all of the body's natural odors; excessive use of deodorants and perfumes destroys the highly erotic smells and flavors that are a part of each individual's distinctiveness.

Fellatio and cunnilingus can be practiced simultaneously in the '69' position, in which the man lies with his head toward his partner's feet and vice versa, enabling each person to reach the other's genital area. Oral kissing can extend to the anal region. The French call such kisses 'rose petals.'

In the '69' position (top and right), partners can pleasure each other simultaneously.

Positions

rehistoric art contains many different images of the woman straddling the male during the sexual act. This position was also dominant during the ancient Greek and Roman civilizations. Anthropologist Bronislaw Malinowski has reported that the natives of the Trobriand Islands, which are attached to Papua New Guinea, make love in a crouching position. Thus, no one position is more 'normal' than another, although the so-called missionary position in all its variations remains the most common in the Western world.

It would no doubt be more logical to say 'missionary positions,' for there are countless variations. The most traditional form, with the woman lying on her back and the man on top, is also the most frequently derided, as if pleasure cannot be had unless the most intricate acrobatics are involved. This position maximizes face-to-face contact (unless the lights are out), breast and pubic contact, and deep kissing. Tongues intertwine, with the rhythm of the breathing matching the cadences of penetration.

Penetration, however, is not very deep. To get around this, the woman can bring her knees up to her partner's chest, then cross her legs around his waist. She can also hook her legs over his shoulders, with a pillow under her buttocks to aid penetration and ensure comfort. Another variation involves her placing her pelvis on the edge of the bed, while the man enters her from a crouching position. Finally, in the classic position, she can squeeze her legs together to regenerate a flagging penis.

There are several ways to reverse the usual missionary position, and it is up to the woman to take matters in hand.

*The classic missionary position
(right, with one variation shown above)
maximizes eye-to-eye contact.*

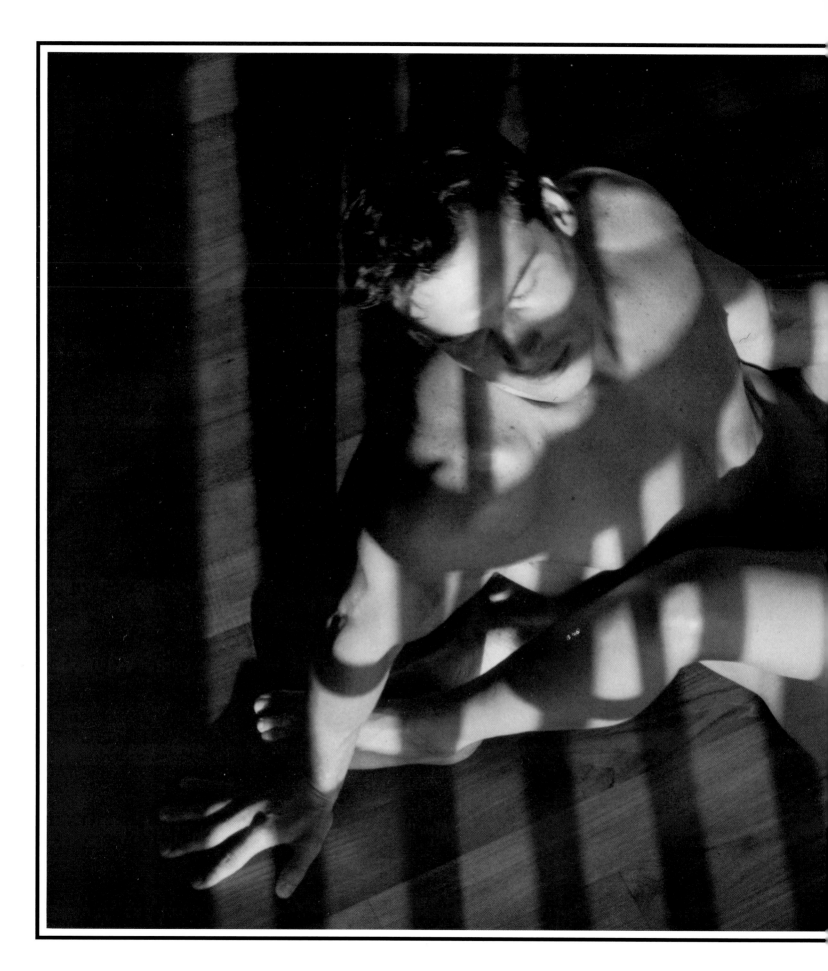

She can spread her legs wide on either side of her partner, or squeeze her legs together and lie between his. She can straddle him vertically, in a half-sitting posture, while leaning on her hands. This enables her to control penetration.

Another possibility is for the couple to lie on their sides, with the woman's legs straddling the man. In this position, he lies back on the bed while his partner is on top, with only her legs resting on him.

There are a whole host of other positions which could be adopted. Performed face to face, standing positions require some practice as they are tiring, and because the penis often slips out of the vagina. One solution is for the woman to cross her legs around her partner's hips. Whatever the method, one of the partners must lean on something solid, such as a table or bathroom sink, in order to remain upright.

A tergo positions are those in which penetration takes place from behind (from the Latin *tergum*, meaning back). They can be performed in various ways: the woman lies on her belly with her partner on top; the man lies on his back, with his partner on top and her back to him; she can be lying or kneeling down, or crouching. (This latter position is known as the Aretin position.) Partners can also lie on their sides, wrapped around each other (the so-called 'gun-dog' position), or the woman can kneel down and turn her back to her partner (the so-called 'doggy' position). This technique maximizes manual stimulation of the clitoris, breasts, and inner thighs.

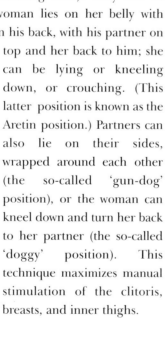

When the man enters the woman from behind, he's able to play with her breasts, clitoris, and inner thighs more easily.

A couple of the straddling and sitting positions have already been described in the earlier section dealing with variations on the missionary position. According to Ovid in his poem *The Art of Love*, the lateral position requires the least effort. For this reason, it is particularly suitable for overweight couples, and for pregnant women. In the sitting position, one of the partners must sit on a chair, on the edge of the bed, or on any surface that is sufficiently solid and comfortable (three-legged stools should therefore be avoided). If the woman is seated, she should lift herself up slightly and lean backward to facilitate penetration. If it is the man in the sitting position, his partner should impale herself on his erection.

If the sitting position is adopted in bed, its greater stability permits a few variations (assuming that is that the couple are sufficiently flexible and practiced): the woman, who is on top, wraps her legs around the man's neck; or, slightly bending her legs, she places her feet on his shoulders. With her feet firmly resting on his shoulders, she can then let herself drop backward while holding onto his hips.

The straddling position can be performed by the woman in different ways: lying across her partner; sitting upright; or crouching while either leaning forward or backward. She supports herself on her hands, which allows her to control the rhythm of the penetration very effectively.

There are many versions of the sitting and straddling positions (shown right and opposite respectively). Whichever you try, make sure you are sitting on something solid!

Orgasms

*The orgasm, derived from the Greek word **orgasmos**, meaning to boil over with ardor, is the most intense and subjective moment of the sexual act. Moans, screams, laughter, contortions, contemplative silence – people experience orgasms differently according to individual sensitivities and experience.*

For men, the moment of orgasm is usually characterized by ejaculation from a full erection. Sexologists, however, encounter patients who complain that they have never experienced a true orgasm, even though they appear to function normally.

Unlike in women, sensorial feeling in men does not always decrease, and muscular contractions are sometimes limited to several propulsions of the male urethra, which can extend to be felt in the muscles of the legs and face. Gasps, cries, shouts, and bodily frenzy are rarely observed in men. Men are rather more 'discreet' in pleasure, with only an occasional grunt, possibly as a result of sociocultural stereotyping that traditionally links virility with the reigning-in of emotion.

For women, however, orgasms are longer but also more diffuse. The clitoris swells, reddens, and becomes turgid while waves of pleasure spread throughout the body, accompanied by spasmodic contractions that are also felt in the sphincter. The vagina, which is already lubricated with desire, becomes swollen and grows deeper as it rhythmically contracts. The end of intercourse is frequently marked by heavy breathing, the loss of sensorial feeling, the abandonment of all thought, and dissolution of the will.

Women often have difficulties reaching an orgasm, and three factors seem to account for this. Orgasm only occurs when arousal is maintained at the same level for a relatively long time. Also, women are infinitely more sensitive to distractions such as bad breath, uncomfortable positions, a prickly beard, and so on. And, finally, sociocultural repression has, historically, discouraged women from reaching orgasm: 'Pleasure is not the concern of honest women,' wrote the otherwise-enlightened French writer Jean Ferrat not too long ago.

Generally, women only reach orgasm when their level of sexual excitement has been maintained for a relatively long time.

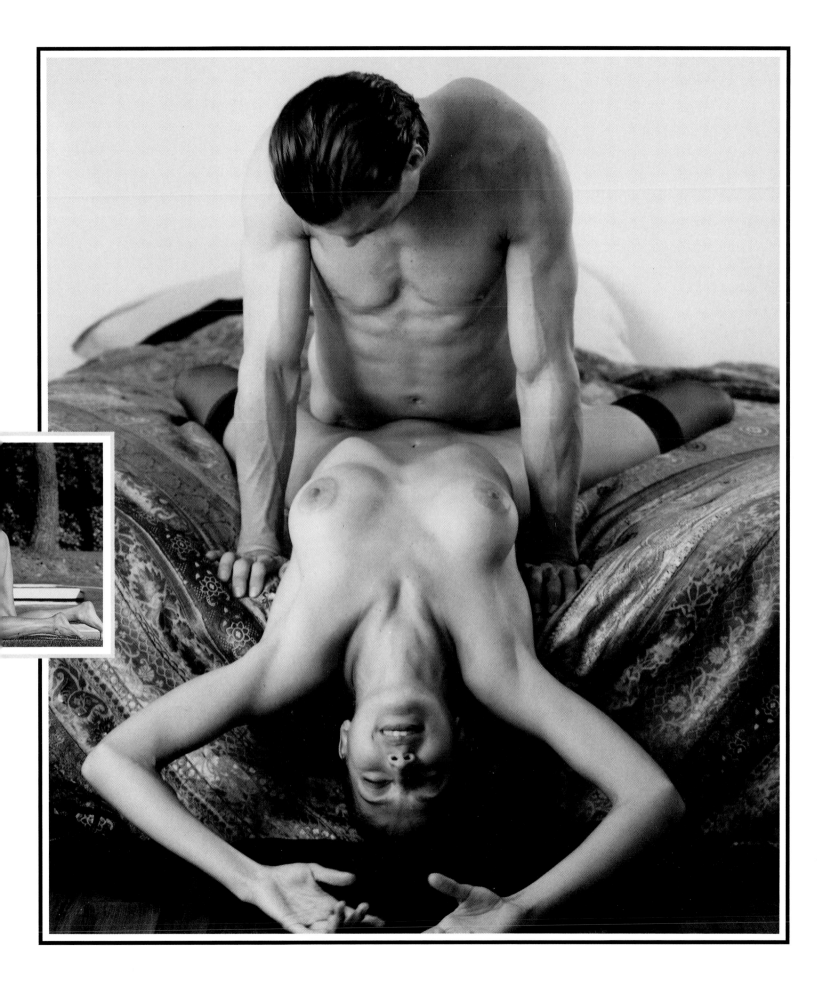

Fantasies and
How to Escape Boredom

A couple's sex life often suffers and becomes boring when both lead busy lives, especially when both partners are faithful to each other. Imagination, fantasy, and inventiveness should be inherent in sexual frolicking, regardless of whether you are enjoying foreplay or full intercourse.

Surprise and spontaneity are indispensable ingredients when a couple are looking for ways to spice up their sexual relationship. A new hair-style, a different hair color, and clothes such as negligees, body suits, garter belts, black corsets, bodices, high heels, and – tastes permitting – whips, may make your partner terribly excited. Although our culture limits the range of erotic clothes and accessories that can be worn by men, donning a smoking jacket or tuxedo for a fine supper with dimmed lights can still be enough to awaken a woman's desire.

Some couples set aside a certain day and time for their sexual rendezvous, and prepare for it mentally and emotionally several days in advance. They anticipate how they will dress, fantasize about what they will say, prepare themselves for what they will do, preferably, for the first time. A 'first time' can simply be a familiar practice for both, with one or two unexpected sequences added.

Some couples play 'fight': bites, scratches, measured punches, and various provocations such as talking about previous lovers or recent flirtations can give these physical reunions a faintly painful pleasure. Others prefer a more languorous and romantic atmosphere with candles, tender whispered words, well-chilled champagne, lace, and even Italian straw hats!

But you can also choose humor – the sound of laughter mingled with gasps of pleasure can be intensely erotic. All games are permissible provided both partners freely consent to them, and so long as they are not physically or mentally harmful.

Unlikely places, disguises, props, play fights: such things can all help to spice up a long-term sexual liaison.

Aphrodisiacs

*T*he word 'aphrodisiac' literally means resembling Aphrodite, the goddess of love and beauty in Greek mythology. According to legend, her erotic aura was so powerful she could bewitch any mortal and make him obey her every whim.

From time immemorial humankind has looked for ways to increase and stimulate its sexual appetite and capacities. The Roman emperor Gallianus, for example, claimed that truffles opened the way to sensuality. Even bananas and, in the Far East, crushed lion's penis and rhinoceros horn were considered powerful aphrodisiacs.

But do aphrodisiacs in fact work? Let us examine the contents of an oyster, one of the most commonly cited examples of an aphrodisiac: 70 to 90 percent consists of water; other constituents include a few proteins and some mineral salt. The truffle is hardly any better: it consists of 70 to 80 percent water, more proteins, and a hint of sugar. Androstenediol, a steroid, has been discovered in truffles, which might explain why they are not mere placebos. But such common chemical substances could only, at best, satisfy a mediocre sexual appetite and then only if consumed in large quantities.

So why has humankind, from antiquity, attributed erogenous powers to these products? The answer perhaps lies in what the Ancients called 'sympathetic magic,' that is to say the resemblance between natural objects, such as fruit, roots, or leaves, and parts of the human body, particularly the sexual organs.

A good example is the mandrake, whose power as an aphrodisiac was celebrated throughout medieval Europe. This Mediterranean herb, a member of the nightshade family, has a strange knobbly root that is strikingly similar to both the man's and the woman's sexual organs. It was believed to promote conception.

The shape and internal consistency of the oyster, meanwhile, are reminiscent of the texture of the vagina's mucous membrane. Similarly, the soft, juicy truffle is a fairly good copy of the penis. As for the banana, it goes without saying ...

This leaves us with the crushed lion's penis and rhinoceros horn, and it would perhaps be appropriate to relate their symbolic importance as aphrodisiacs to the sheer physical strength with which these mammals are seen to mount their females during the mating season.

Fact or fiction? Perhaps the so-called 'power'
of aphrodisiacs says more about the fertility of the
human imagination than about the effectiveness
of the substances themselves.

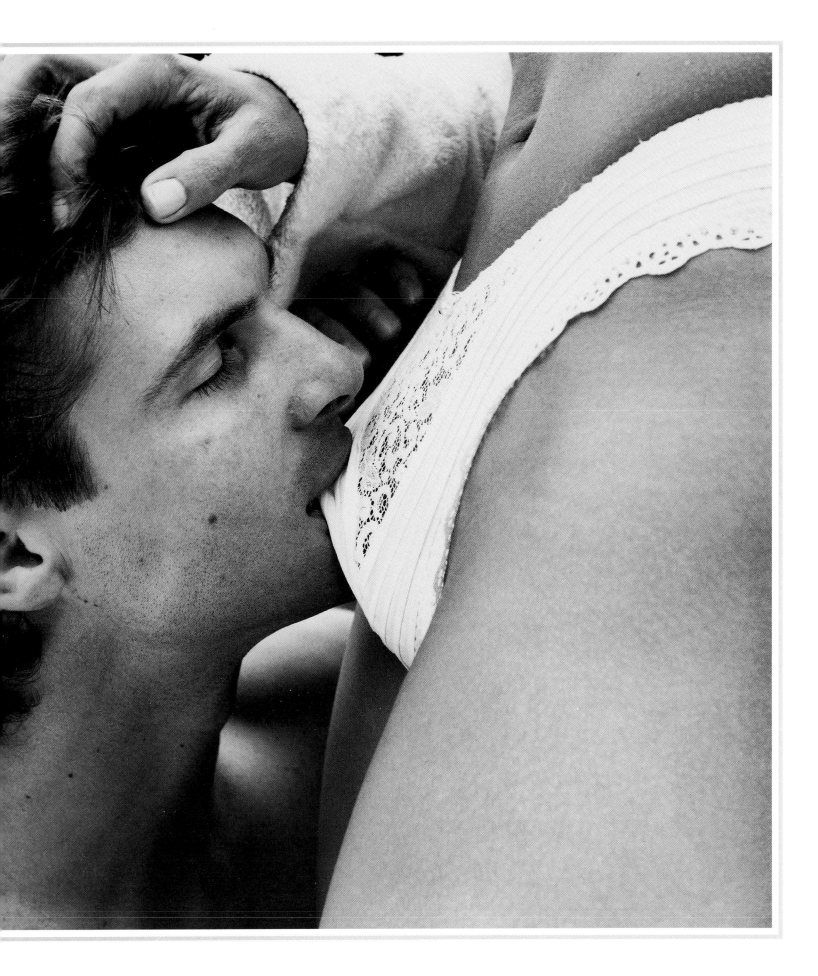

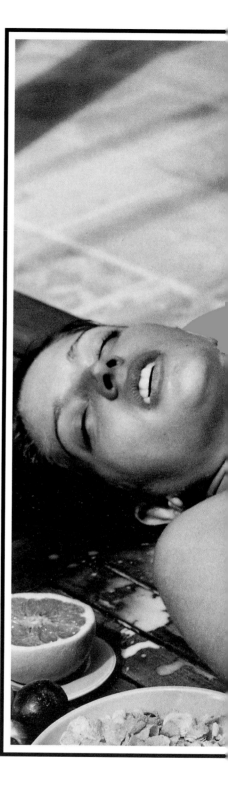

In fact, none of these aphrodisiacs has been proven to work. But alcohol, if consumed in moderate doses, can remove taboos and inhibitions, particularly in women. It dilates the blood vessels, giving a warm sensation of well-being, and it is also a powerful sedative that puts the higher brain region to sleep, hence helping to lift social or moral barriers. In men, excessive drinking makes erection and ejaculation difficult, and chronic alcoholism can lead to impotence.

Of the countless aphrodisiacs mentioned in popular traditions, we shall discuss just two. Cantharides (commonly known as 'Spanish Fly') is a powder extracted from meat-eating flies that live in ash trees throughout the south of Europe and especially in Spain. It affects the membrane lining of the urethra, making it swollen and inflamed. This can give men a long-lasting and powerful erection, with or without sexual desire, and in women can cause an inflamed, tense sensation that will drive her to seek relief through sexual intercourse. But there are, however, bad side effects, including severe inflammation of the stomach and intestines, or internal bleeding and even dangerous lesions of the kidneys and intestines.

The second substance is yohimbine, an alkaloid extracted from the bark of the yohimbehe tree, which grows in central Africa. The locals use it in its pure, crystalline state to cure sexual problems and, in particular, impotence. But its effects on the spinal cord require that it be used only with the greatest caution. Experts conclude, therefore, that these two substances are not true aphrodisiacs, in the correct sense, which should of course be completely safe to use, as well as erogenous.

Some substances used to improve
sexual performance – cantharides
and yohimbine, for example –
can have dangerous side-effects,
and should be avoided.

Sodomy

nal sex requires tenderness and consensus; otherwise it has no place in the lovemaking ritual. You must also be aware of local legislation because some states and countries outlaw this intimate act.

Anal intercourse is best practiced after the woman has been thoroughly aroused by means of vaginal caressing. A finger is inserted in the well-lubricated vagina; the fully lubricated finger can then be used to stimulate the anus and perineum. (The perineum is the little bridge of muscles and flesh linking the anus to the scrotum in men and the anus to the vulva in women. It is particularly sensitive to touch, which heightens the quality of anal intercourse.) Always wear a condom when practicing anal sex; never enter the vagina immediately after anal intercourse even if you are wearing a condom. The rectum, which is the prolongation of the anus and part of the large intestine, contains germs harmful to the equilibrium of the vagina. This precaution should be observed with manual caressing as well. It is also advised that sodomy not be practiced regularly, as the anal sphincter, which was not designed for this use, may stretch.

A couple's love life is very private and personal and the decision to participate in anal sex should be a joint one. If one partner is unwilling or unresponsive the resulting bad feeling could ultimately damage an otherwise loving and perhaps very important relationship.

There are a variety of positions for anal sex (above and right).

Fantasies and Perversions

*T*he word 'fantasy' was first used in 1836 and was defined as 'a medical term' – 'a visual or sometimes mental lesion in which the ill believe they see objects when there is nothing in front of them.'

Fantasy replaces frustration with imaginary satisfaction and is the essential element in masturbation, for example. Fantasy frequently involves people who are absent from you – your usual partner, or somebody whom you are attracted to, perhaps an acquaintance, friend, or celebrity. But most often, fantasies involve unusual situations that spice up the daydreamer's emotions. Women who ordinarily condemn rape sometimes dream about brutal and passionate intercourse with a stranger or with somebody who is totally opposite in character to the men they are usually attracted to. Shy, reserved men often fantasize about having the courage to conquer the most inaccessible women.

Almost all fantasies are based on some sadomasochistic drive that psychologists say is present in all of us. Fantasies are outlets for unfulfilled desires, and they allow us to pretend we are someone else and to turn the tables on reality. A man who is usually shy and introverted might fantasize about sadistic scenes in which he is dominating and aggressive. A mild-mannered woman who is considered very feminine by her friends may only be able to climax by fantasizing about (and sometimes initiating) rough sex and torture scenarios with her partner.

Most of the time, however, fantasies are completely harmless: imaginary scenarios used to relieve impulses that we are unable to put into practice.

Fantasy plays a crucial role in a healthy sex life, whether during masturbation (right) or as part of outdoor sex (above).

Erotic Accessories

Erotic photos and books, X-rated movies, and suggestive lingerie – there are numerous accessories that provoke and reinforce sexuality. Your choice of accessories is a question of taste and imagination.

With a little bit of imagination, just about anything can inflame anyone's sexual desire. Black stockings, high-heeled shoes, and fur have become associated with sex because they are often used during lovemaking. They have become fetishized, a word derived from the Portuguese term *feitiço*, meaning 'charm.'

In everyday language, a fetish is an object to which supernatural and beneficial properties are unconsciously attributed by its owner. This type of fixation begins in childhood or adolescence and is often triggered by a visual shock linked to a libidinal emotion: a scene in a movie, for example, in which a woman undoes her stocking from her garter may give an adolescent boy his first erection. From then on, he may need to re-create this experience with his sexual partners in order to become excited.

Sexual devices, like aphrodisiacs (see page 68), are designed to ignite sexual energy. For some people, more often men than women, sex without them becomes dull and insipid, and then, finally, inconceivable.

Some articles of clothing not only stimulate erotic interest but also act as symbols of sexual organs. Love is a theater, and on the stage of desire, anything is possible; a stiletto heel is sometimes wielded like a penis, and the inside of a shoe probed like a vagina. And lingerie is often used to showcase a woman's body, to accentuate its many exquisite jewels: breasts held in a strapless brassiere, the pubis framed by lace garters, buttocks snared in G-string panties.

More or less anything can be used as an erotic accessory, from shoes to candles, lingerie to mirrors: the only limits are those imposed by your own imagination.

Water Games

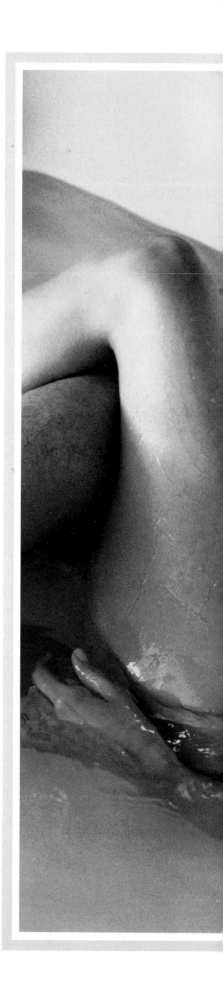

*C*hildren discover the pleasure of water at a very young age. From an early age bath-time is associated with games and with our mothers' tender caresses, and reminds us of how warm and comfortable it was in the womb. These first experiences leave indelible marks on adult sexuality.

The bath can be a long and voluptuous prelude to intercourse, which can itself take place in the water. When you plan to share a bath with your partner, everything must be well-prepared; nothing should be left to chance. You should check the temperature of the water (it should be warm, but not too hot) and perhaps add bubble bath or delicately scented oils. Scatter a few flowers or petals to the water to add to the special atmosphere.

Massage either cream or perfumed oils onto each other's bodies before slipping into the water. Let the nipples and the penis glide over glistening skin. Take your time and slowly, seductively wash your partner's body. Then it will be your turn to relax and enjoy the same sensual sensation.

And you can have fun drying each other off, teasing each other with gentle tickling and paying special attention to those parts of the body susceptible to pleasure: the breasts, genitalia, buttocks – and even each other's feet.

Warm, scented water and soft, glistening skin: make the most of the delights of bath-time by playing voluptuous games – the perfect prelude to full intercourse.

Pornography and Eroticism

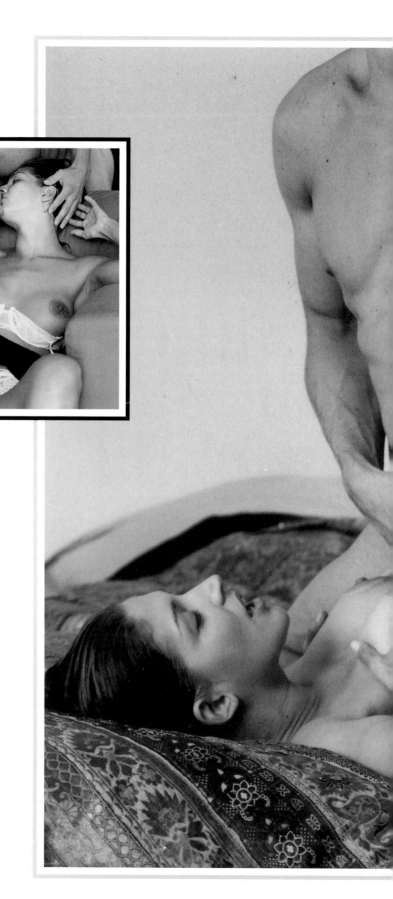

The word 'pornography' is a combination of the Greek words **pornê**, meaning prostitute, and **graphein**, meaning to write.

Dictionaries define pornography as obscene art or literature. The word 'obscenity' itself is derived from the Latin word *obscenus*, meaning something that does not augur well, or an act or object that offends modesty. The word eroticism, on the other hand, refers to Eros, the Greek god of erotic love, and the well-known symbol of desire and pleasure.

The boundary between pornography and erotica is difficult to determine. The difference between the two is really a political matter, dependent on social consensus and the prevailing cultural attitudes of the time. Nevertheless, the term 'pornography' has negative connotations in comparison to 'erotica,' which enjoys a more ennobled status.

Eroticism is the description and glorification of physical love. Pornography, on the other hand, is frequently tainted by 'dirtiness,' strangeness, and abnormality. Pornography caters to impulses generally perceived as perverse, such as scatology, masochism, and sadism. And, although these distinctions may seem arbitrary to some people, it should always be remembered that some sexual practices can never be tolerated under any circumstances; rape or any other kind of abuse is never permissible.

What some couples find erotic may seem repulsive to others – age, upbringing, and the culture of the country in which we are raised serve to shape and define what we find erotic. Definitions of pornography are similarly variable. But one factor is clear – erotic behavior (and erotica) is consensual and inclusive whereas pornography is not.

While eroticism celebrates human sexuality and the shared joy and happiness it brings to partners, pornography panders to our sub-rational fascination with the solely physical aspects of sex.

Woods, a deserted beach next to a lagoon, a discreet thicket of leafy trees in an abandoned park – these are just a few of the multitude of secluded places that are ideal for making love. And making love outdoors has the added thrill of the possibility of being caught in the act.

There is not a more ideal setting for lovemaking than a quiet, secluded spot, fanned by gentle breezes and washed with the pungent scent of pine trees. But nature has some inconveniences; take along a blanket or thick towel to protect yourself from pine needles, sand, pebbles, or ants.

As fornication in a public place is prohibited by law, however, you should take care not to be surprised in the act by any persons of authority. Watch out for voyeurs, as well, although they are usually not dangerous; studies show that voyeurs are anxious and insecure about their own virility. Watching others often reassures voyeurs and arouses them.

Making love outdoors stimulates the mind and body alike. Take care where you do it, though – it is against the law in many countries.

CHAPTER 3

Love

*I*f love were the same for everybody, it would be pointless to search for its specific meaning, its essence. All we would need to do is to let ourselves go and lose ourselves in its depths. But love, as the saying goes, is a many-splendored thing. It represents an infinity of sensations, a vast and varied array of passions, desires, and states of consciousness. Despot and savior, liberator and destroyer, it is the guiding force of existence, the ultimate ruler of all human behavior.

Sexual relations in prehistoric times were performed under the yoke of oppressive biological needs. Coitus was reached *a tergo*, from behind, a position favorable to penetration and procreation. Libidinal attraction was olfactory; like dogs, human beings were ruled by pheromones, chemical substances secreted by the gonads that attract and keep sexual partners. Since then, the human mind has enhanced sexuality, transforming it into a marvelous and enduring adventure that sustains itself through the imagination. We have learned that, as adults, we can love each other with the same intense spiritual and tender affection that children feel for their mothers, and mothers for their children. The bonds of adult love are rooted in and constantly perfected and reinvented through this willful imagining.

*Love, tenderness, imagination, and fantasy
should all be part of the sexual act –
if it is to be truly fulfilling.*

Is Masturbation the Prelude to Romantic Encounters?

From the Latin words manus, meaning 'hand', and stupro, 'to pollute', masturbation is an autoerotic activity that enables the individual to achieve pleasurable sensations, and orgasm, through the stimulation of the genital organs.

The notion of 'polluted hand' shows how much this practice is scorned. The English social anthropologist Desmond Morris recalls in his book, *Intimate Behavior*, how children and adolescents were punished when caught masturbating:

> *Young delinquent boys were made to wear a silver ring in their foreskin. The clitoris of young girls was sometimes mutilated through either surgical cauterization or the complete removal of the clitoris. Once they reached puberty, adolescents of both sexes frequently had to sleep with their hands tied together or to the bed.*

A variation of this practice continued in some boarding schools until the end of the 19th century; young girls were frequently forced to sleep with both arms outside the bed covers. If anybody was caught contravening this rule, they would be immediately awakened and punished.

This century – thanks in no small part to Freud's teachings – it has gradually come to be accepted that in fact there is nothing more natural and infantile than masturbation: children discover it at an extremely young age. From adolescence onward, masturbation often becomes the prelude to all sexual activity. The pleasurable sensations it produces make the genital organs and the entire body sensitive to lovemaking with a partner. Be careful, however, that masturbation does not become a substitute for a full sexual relationship with a loving partner.

There is nothing wrong or 'unnatural' about masturbation. It can be a gentle way for couples to 'warm up' before lovemaking.

Erotic Daydreams

In erotic daydreams, particular scenarios are often repeated. These daydreams are filled with fleeting images and memories of past sexual encounters. Erotic daydreams can also keep sexual desire alive.

Erotic daydreamers often fantasize about the same people playing the same role. Their actions may change, but they always submit to the will of the dreamer.

Fantasies, like nocturnal dreams, are healthy because they enable the dreamer to satisfy what is often an unconscious desire. According to Freud, sexual instinct is made up of partial impulses that may be fetishistic, exhibitionistic, voyeuristic, sadistic, or masochistic in nature. Fantasies are symbolic outlets for these impulses. Freud always insisted on the profound need of human beings to reconstitute the familiar triangle of father, mother, and child. This is called the oedipal triangle in reference to the oedipal complex, which describes a child's libidinal attraction to the parent of the opposite sex.

Sadomasochistic fantasies also occupy a privileged position in the pantheon of erotic daydreams. Rape fantasies are preponderant among women, but this is not to mean that women actually want to be raped; women fantasize about being forced into sensual abandonment in a way that they would certainly disapprove of in real life.

Tying a woman to the bed so that she is at her partner's mercy, as in Pedro Almodovar's movie, *Tie Me Up, Tie Me Down*, is also a favorite fantasy theme for men. Conversely, men dream of being forced to submit to the terrible whims of a dominatrix.

Other popular fantasies include partner-swapping and homosexual encounters – erotic daydreams know no boundaries. They allow the libido to run loose, to express itself freely, without jeopardizing the couple, or the moral standards that they share.

Erotic daydreams are healthy, even if they involve situations which the dreamer would find repugnant in real life.

The Laughter of Love

*T*he problem with most eroticism is that it takes itself too seriously, with its ripped bodices and high-flung passions, panting lovers, and shuddering, world-shattering climaxes. While this vision of love is not entirely incorrect, it can be somewhat off-putting, especially when it is taken as a model for all romantic relationships.

We sometimes forget the role humor can play in lovemaking. Laughter in this context is too often misconstrued as mockery, brought on by some ridiculous aspect of our behavior or bodies, such as a pimple, wart, comical expression, or a high-pitched squeak made during a moment of passion. But laughter can just as easily be an expression of joy and pleasure, a celebration of sensation, an extraordinary lightness of being that is evoked by touch and tongue, by the pleasure of kiss or caress.

Psychotherapists know the power of laughter and the essential role it plays in the healing process; laughing restores the sufferer's taste for life and helps him or her to overcome the pain and despair brought on by illness. Business consultants use comedy as a means to alleviate stress and improve interpersonal relations. During role-playing exercises, for example, participants are invited to tell funny stories, perform stand-up routines, and take part in 'laugh-therapy,' which all help relieve tension and create stronger ties between colleagues.

The loving laugh provides us with another means to approach the erotic. Laughter allows us to break down the walls between partners and to 'melt the ice,' to bring a joyous and complex-free levity to the act of love.

Sex can be taken too seriously: the ability to laugh at aspects of our own behavior will help our partner to relax, creating a warm, loving atmosphere.

Pregnancy and Sexuality

*N*owadays, it is still widely believed that women should forgo sexual intercourse during pregnancy so as not to traumatize the fetus and risk abortion. However, there is no medical reason for avoiding sexual activity during pregnancy if the woman is in good health and the pregnancy is progressing normally.

There are three distinct cycles governing a pregnant woman's sexual appetite. During the first trimester, most future mothers experience a drop in sexual desire and satisfaction. This is due to fatigue, sleepiness, nausea, and other discomforting physical conditions. Women also fear that sexual intercourse will harm the uterus and traumatize the fetus. Sometimes pregnancy has a negative effect on the mental and sexual equilibrium of couples; the man may be jealous of the fetus, causing the woman to react defensively to what she perceives as aggression or indifference on the part of her partner.

Some couples, therefore, give up sexual activity until after the child's birth. Unfortunately, this sexual abstinence can become habitual as a family routine becomes established and the couple adopts parental roles.

During the second trimester, many women regain their sexual appetite. As their libido becomes stronger, their sexual satisfaction increases. During this time, men should be careful in choosing positions that are not too strenuous for their partner (see Chapter Four *Questions and Answers*, page 136).

In the third trimester, sexual activity usually decreases because the woman tires easily. By this time, she is quite heavy and many movements can be painful for her. It is also likely that she has begun to anticipate nursing her baby and that her attention is no longer focused on sex.

The most significant risk in carrying on sexual activity during pregnancy is that contractions may lead to abortion. Therefore, medical consultation is advised.

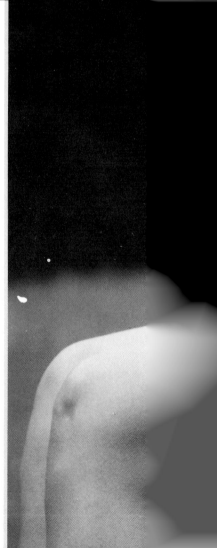

In most cases, pregnant women can continue to have sex. Choose a comfortable position and, if in any doubt, consult a physician.

Sexually-Transmitted Diseases

*V*enereal diseases (from Venus, the god of love) are problems that all sexually active people may encounter at some point in their lives. They are often unjustly subject to moral judgment; some sexually-transmitted diseases, like other illnesses, can be cured with medical treatment, sometimes supplemented by psychological counseling.

Gonorrhea is caused by a germ and appears from one to five days after infection. In men, it causes a frequent need to urinate and a burning sensation during urination. In women, gonorrhea may cause a white discharge and a slight burning sensation during urination, but can be symptomless.

Herpes is a virus that results in the outbreak of clusters of small sores full of clear liquid on the face, generally around the corners of the lips, or on the genitalia. These can be accompanied by fever, various aches and pains similar to flu symptoms, and eye strain. Trichomonas are parasitic organisms that are usually transmitted through sexual activity, but also through toiletry items. They cause vaginal infection in women, which is characterized by a greenish-colored, often putrid discharge. In men, they can also cause a discharge from the penis, and discomfort when urinating.

Syphilis is a serious disease transmitted by sexual contact as well as soiled objects. The discovery of antibiotics has greatly reduced the significance of this disease, once nicknamed 'the pox.' Syphilis develops in three stages: it begins with an incubation period of three weeks characterized by the appearance of chancres, or hard ulcers; secondary symptoms appear about two months later and include fever, malaise, and a faint red rash on the chest. Months or even years later, deep lesions can appear and cause serious damage to the cardiovascular and nervous systems.

Viral hepatitis A and B are also sexually-transmitted diseases. These infections are characterized by necrosis, or tissue death, and inflammation of the liver. Hepatitis A can be transmitted orally and through sexual contact; hepatitis B is transmitted by infected blood or sexual contact.

And finally, there is AIDS or Acquired Immune Deficiency Syndrome. AIDS symptoms are those that occur in patients whose natural defense mechanisms no longer function normally. The AIDS virus tends to attack the digestive system, lungs, and the brain (see Chapter Four *Questions and Answers*, pages 154–155). To minimize the chance of catching the AIDS virus, always practice safe sex with a new partner, with the male or female wearing a condom.

It is not worth taking a chance –
always practice safe sex with a new partner.

Breasts

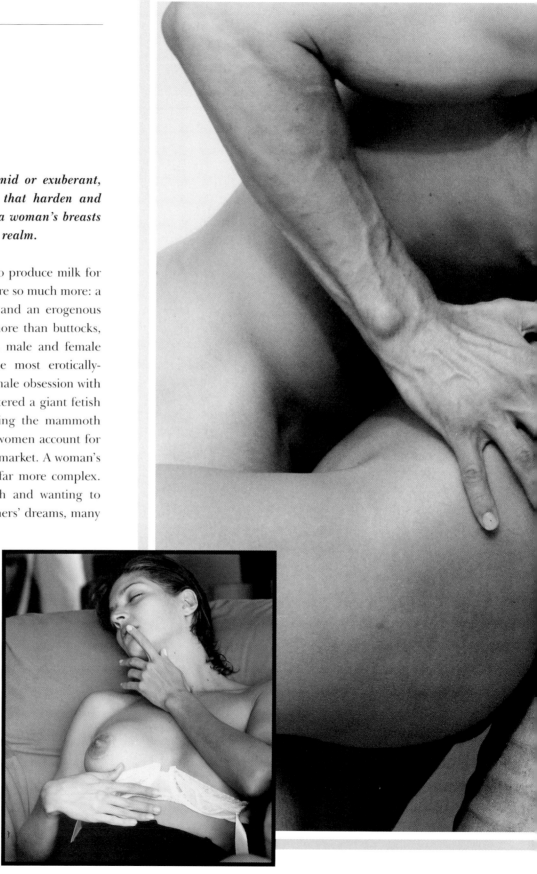

*P*ert or generous, large or small, timid or exuberant, pear-shaped or conical, with nipples that harden and push out or remain dimpled and soft, a woman's breasts hold a privileged position in the sexual realm.

The primary function of the breasts is to produce milk for the nourishment of newborns, but they are so much more: a symbol of femininity, an erotic charm, and an erogenous zone. In Western civilization, breasts, more than buttocks, the pubis, or legs, have forever fueled male and female fantasies. For most men, they are the most erotically-charged parts of the female body. The male obsession with breasts – the bigger the better – has fostered a giant fetish industry; magazines and films celebrating the mammoth mammaries of extremely well-endowed women account for a huge proportion of the pornographic market. A woman's relationship to her breasts, however, is far more complex. Dissatisfied with too little or too much and wanting to become the woman of their own and others' dreams, many turn to plastic surgery.

From a purely biological point of view, male and female breasts are identical. Transsexuals take female hormones to develop fuller breasts. The breast is a milk-secreting gland surrounded by fatty tissue. Its capacity to lactate after childbirth is uninfluenced by its size.

The breasts are one of the most sensitive of the erogenous zones: oral and tactile stimulation of the nipples can lead some women to orgasm.

Forever and Ever ...

'The law of love is hard, but no matter how unjust,
it must be obeyed, for since the beginning of time,
it alone has brought together the heavens and the earth.'
(Francesco Petrarch, 14th-century Italian poet)

No word carries as much weight, or causes so much confusion, as the word 'love.' We love our wives and husbands, but we also love baseball, apple pie, and root beer. How are these loves so very different?

Initially, we love in the manner we were loved as a child. Those people who were denied love as children, or who did not receive adequate affection or attention, often scare away partners by moving too fast, by being too hungry for love, too intrusive, and too demanding. Those people who were smothered with maternal love tend to seek out partners who respect their need for space, and who give them the breathing room they were denied as children.

Any relationship, no matter how 'loving,' can never be entirely harmonious, as both partners follow the dictates of a different set of unconscious needs and drives. 'I love you more than you love me' is a phrase that is commonly thought, if not always expressed. Suffering, so very often an essential component of love, arises from this conflict between these neurotic demands, and only patience and frankness can help to overcome them.

Individuals who did not receive enough affection when they were children tend to be over-demanding in their adult relationships.

In addition, cultural norms demand that 'true' love be both exclusive and exclusively sexual. This is far from being the case. One person can be head over heels in love with another without ever having or even wanting to make love to him or her, while another might enter into sexual relations with several different partners without ever giving his or her heart or making any type of emotional investment. And, very often, two people will create an intense emotional bond, but find that their lovemaking is unfulfilling.

Of course, two people can also share an emotional and physical love that is absolute and unshakeable. Why is this so rare? What causes a man, wild with desire for the woman of his dreams, to go limp the moment she offers herself to him? What causes a woman, totally devoted to her knight in shining armor, to remain unmoved and distant when he makes love to her?

Most psychosexual dysfunctions originate in an inability to recognize the integral part the libido plays in the human condition. Angels and devils, madonnas and whores, society hides the uncontrollable power of love behind a flimsy facade of stereotypes and convention. Fortunately love, whether sexual or platonic, passionate or affectionate, celestial or terrestrial, will conquer all.

Despite what some movies, books, and magazines tell us, no relationship can ever be entirely harmonious, however deeply in love the couple may be.

Did You Know?

According to the *Anangaranga*, the 16th-century erotic masterpiece written by the Indian king Kalyanamalla, scratching is a powerful erotic stimulus for the female libido. 'Mayûrapâda,' the peacock's foot, is achieved by tracing a line with fingernails and thumbnail around the nipple. 'Cchurita,' the graze, is a light, delicate scratch with a single nail across the cheeks, lower lip, or the breasts.

According to the World Health Organization, there are 5.5 billion active lovemakers on the planet, and 200 million acts of intercourse every day. This results in 910,000 births a day, of which 25 percent are unwanted, and 365,000 cases of sexually-transmitted infections.

In a university study, an equal number of American men and women watched several hours of pornographic films. All of the men in the group said that the material had excited them physically, while only 50 percent of the women said the same. However, the entire group had been monitored electronically, and all exhibited heightened physiological excitement – including those who professed to be left cold.

In her book *The Natural History of Love*, Helen Fisher, citing a United Nations study on 62 different cultures, observes that most divorces occur during the fourth year of marriage. This is true regardless of age, profession, or the local belief system.

According to the World Health Organization, some 200 million acts of sexual intercourse take place every day, world-wide.

The History of Desire

'*In this world there are only two tragedies. One is not getting what one wants, and the other is getting it.*' (*Oscar Wilde, LADY WINDERMERE'S FAN*)

Romantic and sexual love are expressed in different ways. From a strictly biological point of view, some authors reduce them to a simple hormonal reaction, to a sort of 'biological' love. According to this interpretation, the hypothalamus supervises the force of sexual desire, controls seduction, and is responsible for what is called the lovers' 'state of mind.' The limbic system, or emotional brain, coordinates the sentimental and sensual aspects of sexual relations, stores emotional events into its memory, and is the epicenter of orgasmic pleasure. The neocortex, or higher brain, assures the outcome of intercourse and is responsible for fantasies and erotic imagination, as well as taboos, guilt, and all kinds of self-censorship.

Some experts believe that desire is a purely mental force arising from unsatisfied needs. It is fueled by obstacles and prohibitions and is exacerbated when repressed. When fulfilled, imagined pleasure disappears, and desire along with it. But a tinge of dissatisfaction ensures that desire will rise again, like the phoenix from the ashes.

Desire is a vital force that brings color and intensity to our emotional life, feelings, and passions. It shapes our behavior and tendencies, and our personalities are formed by its incessant ebb and flow.

According to Sigmund Freud, desire is the attachment of the unconscious to early experiences in breast-feeding. Nourishment is linked to the breast (or the bottle) and is enriched by contact with the mother, her scent, and her tender voice. Infantile, adolescent, and adult desire grows increasingly complex but is always linked to these initial infantile experiences.

Desire first manifests itself physically, but is perpetuated in the realm of the mind through the development of imaginary representations that enrich these first sexual experiences.

There are many theories about what 'causes' desire, but one thing is clear: desire is a vital force that brings color to our emotional life.

CHAPTER 4

Questions and Answers — First Sexual Encounters

At what age do first sexual encounters usually occur? Is sex tiring?
What contraception methods are available? It is true that men do not need foreplay?
You can never be too curious when it comes to questions of initiation to sexual fulfillment.
Here's how to discover the keys to the gates of pleasure.

◆ *How important is the first sexual experience? What impact can it have on future sexual relations?*

The initial experience is an important conditioning factor in a person's sexual development. Premature ejaculation, a common problem among males, is linked as much to the circumstances of a man's first sexual encounter as to his libidinal fixations during infancy. His first sexual experience might have taken place in a car or at his companion's home while her parents were out. His constant fear of their being caught in the act may have resulted in an ejaculatory reflex and the beginning of a sexual pattern of premature ejaculation. Girls, whose sensuality is more 'peripheral' than that of boys, usually need more tenderness, attention, and gentleness that first time. If the first encounter is clumsy or too quick, fails to include foreplay, or involves violence, girls can easily be put off sex – and can even come to be repulsed by the thought of it, later on. It is important for young

Do you have to love before making love ?

For the first sexual experience to be happy and enjoyable, the couple should know, and trust, each other – and should feel safe and secure physically.

women and men to begin their sexual life with a partner whom they love or, failing that, with someone who they at least care for or are truly attracted to. This is true for young women, who must deal with the issue of the hymen. Only a sensitive, nonaggressive sexual approach can allay a woman's fear of tearing and perforation. It is important that couples, especially young unmarried ones, discuss the method of contraception they are going to use before sex, as unwanted pregnancies can substantially alter sexual relations, whether between the partners involved or future partners.

◆ Is sex tiring?

Sex is certainly less tiring than most athletic activities. It requires less energy than walking up a flight of stairs, for instance. At the moment of orgasm, the level of adrenalin, a chemical-mediating substance released by the adrenal glands, climbs dramatically, just as it does when one senses danger. The heartbeat and breathing accelerate and vascularization increases, causing a feeling of fatigue. At the same time, the brain secretes endogenous morphine, endorphins, and enkephalins. These substances are closely related to opium, which is one of the strongest analgesics, or painkillers, available. It is due to these substances that we experience feelings of plenitude, calm, relaxation, and drowsiness, while, paradoxically, our minds remain clear and alert. The sexual response cycle consists of four stages: the excitement stage, the plateau stage, orgasm, and resolution. The plateau stage can continue for a very short or long period of time. The period following orgasm is also called the afterglow, when feelings of deep satisfaction and contentment are experienced; this can cause men especially to fall asleep, which may leave the woman feeling rejected and unappreciated.

Is 14 too early an age to start having sexual relationships?

Physiologically speaking, there is no reason why a physically mature girl of 14 cannot begin having sexual relations. However, a girl of this age rarely possesses the mental maturity that is necessary in any enduring relationship. It is therefore best to wait a few years.

◆ What is the average age at which sexual encounters first occur?

This depends on a country's culture, myths, and rituals. These factors also determine when coming of age begins. In western Europe, first sexual relations occur, on average, between the ages of 16 and 20 years for females, and between the ages of 16 and 18 for males. But perhaps it would be more useful to ask whether there is an ideal age at which to start having sexual relations. The end of puberty, when the voice begins to change and secondary sex characteristics such as breasts, hairiness, and penis size are fully developed, could be considered as a 'natural' time to begin sexual relations. However, this does not take into account psychic, cognitive, and intellectual maturity, which does not necessarily develop at the same pace as the body. A 14-year-old girl who began menstruating at age 11 may have the body of a mature woman, but it is unlikely that her behavior, speech, and ideas about existence and the meaning of life have reached a comparable stage of maturity. Moreover, except in certain African and Asian countries, pregnancy at this age, although possible from a strictly physiological point of view, is rarely viewed as normal or ordinary in female sexual development and is recognized as having difficult consequences in the future. The age of both puberty and first sexual encounters has seen a fall in recent years and it has been estimated that 50 percent of teenagers are now sexually active by the age of 16, and 70 percent by 19 years; this has resulted in a rise in the number of teenage pregnancies, especially in western Europe and the USA. Better diet, housing conditions, and advances in medicine are probably responsible for the fall in age at puberty, but the media and more liberal attitudes for the age of first sexual intercourse have also had an effect.

Is it normal for children to masturbate?

According to Freud, masturbation is a natural and basic human function. Sexologists today acknowledge the positive value of masturbation, while warning that, for adults, it should not be indulged in to the exclusion of other forms of sexual activity.

◆ *Can masturbation cause mental or physical damage?*

From the early 19th century to the beginning of the 20th century, many doctors, influenced by contemporary religious beliefs, viewed masturbation as a source of criminal activity and the cause of physical and mental illnesses. At the turn of the century the English sexologist Havelock Ellis published a study that identified all the illnesses that were attributable to masturbation. They included: migraines, deafness, nosebleeds, warts, neuralgia, incontinence, and the sagging of young women's breasts, to name just a few. In 1829, Sir William Ellis, director of the Nanwel asylum in England, peremptorily declared, 'For the majority of our asylum inmates, illness must be attributed to this cause.' However, few sexual behaviors are as widespread as masturbation among animal species. Dogs, cats, baboons, elephants, porcupines, and rodents masturbate quite frequently. Porcupines masturbate with their mouths and paws, and during the rutting season (between September and October), deers rub their highly sensitive antlers against the grass, causing rapid erection and ejaculation.

Freud hypothesized that masturbation was one of the primordial human functions; he saw it as being a kind of primitive need, stronger even than man's seeming need for alcohol and tobacco (which are actually nothing more than 'replacement products' sublimating sexual desire). More recent studies – for example those conducted by Masters and Johnson – acknowledge the wholly positive value of masturbation. Brecher, an American researcher who follows the work of Masters and Johnson very closely, writes in his book, *Sexologists:*

The future of sexuality in our civilization depends less on a college or university education than on a climate that allows children to be self-confident and fully self-accepting, to acknowledge their bodies and sexual impulses. They should be able to masturbate freely, without shame or guilt …

Today, masturbation is the target of a more subtle kind of repression than in earlier times. Parents and educators claim to accept it, but with reservations. Cause and effect are confounded in theories claiming that masturbation causes timidity, fatigue, and introversion. In fact, it is rather that most people masturbate when they are tired, and not the other way around. In short, masturbation is a healthy act when used in lovemaking, or when necessitated by the temporary absence of the partner.

Masturbation should not, however, be allowed to become an exclusive practice, as it cuts the individual off from the very essence of sexuality – the relationship, a word that is derived from the Latin verb *religare*, meaning 'to connect.'

◆ Does the breaking of the hymen always cause bleeding and the loss of virginity? Is it always painful?

It is still common to hear that the deflowering process is very painful, and that it causes bleeding. In fact, in 70 percent of cases, the pain is minimal, and there is only slight blood flow, which usually stops after a few minutes. Women with very elastic hymens will not experience pain or bleeding the first time they have sexual intercourse. The hymen can also be accidentally ripped, for example when women are playing sport. On such occasions, the breaking of the hymen often goes unnoticed. A lack of bleeding during intercourse often convinces the male that his first-time partner is not a virgin, but that is not necessarily the case.

Are orgasms the same for men and women?

It generally takes longer for a woman to become aroused, and, when she has an orgasm, the effects are felt over the whole body, not just in the genital region. The male sexual appetite is more easily aroused. However, erotic dissatisfaction and the inability to reach orgasm are common to both men and women.

◆ Is it true that men do not need foreplay?

It is clear that the prehistoric men in Jean-Jacques Annaud's film *Quest for Fire* did not find foreplay necessary. All it took was a whiff of their females' scent to make them quickly and frenetically mount them from behind. Customs have changed significantly since the era depicted in Annaud's film, however, and except for rapists, drunken brutes, and other modern 'missing links,' men have refined their approach considerably.

It is true, nevertheless, that while male desire is more or less phallocentric and quickly satisfied, female desire, which is not so immediately focussed on the genital area, is slower to awake, and much more diffuse. However, most men, once they realize that sexual foreplay is the only way to ensure that a woman's sexual pleasure coincides with their own, soon discover that the mysterious female body is not alone in its capacity to respond to caressing. For men, just like women, have entirely erogenous bodies.

Basically, foreplay includes the kissing, cuddling, touching, and caressing that takes place between two people prior to intercourse; it is not essential for successful lovemaking, but it can help to make the act of sexual intercourse more meaningful and enjoyable for both partners.

It can start some considerable time before intercourse, perhaps with the planning of a romantic evening or dinner. Foreplay will include getting to know and understand your partner's body; men as well as women like to be desired and admired. Erogenous zones are the parts of the body that are the most sensitive to stimulation and one enjoyable part of foreplay can be to discover your partner's most erogenous zones. Foreplay need not necessarily end in sexual intercourse.

◆ How important is a man's penis size to women?

This is purely a matter of personal taste and preference for the woman concerned. Statistics on this question, published in a report by Masters and Johnson, reveal a wide variety of preferences. Yet many age-old myths still prevail – that women prefer very large penises, for example. This unfounded theory has in turn sprouted several racist and xenophobic offshoots. For example, some Western men accuse supposedly better-endowed men belonging to non-Caucasian ethnic groups of 'stealing' their women, a theory once propagated by the Ku Klux Klan. In fact, sexologists and gynecologists find that many of their patients are wary of overly imposing penises. For some women, they render intercourse painful, even impossible. (These women, even if they have given birth, forget that the vaginal passage is extremely flexible.) And as for those worried about the 'effectiveness' of smaller penises, it should be stressed that, as the vaginal erogenous zones are less than two inches from the vulva, the length of the penis contributes very little to female sexual pleasure.

◆ Can a woman have sex during her period?

Here again, sexual preferences and prejudices are the sole arbiters of what a couple may or may not do when the woman is menstruating. Many men, especially those who are in love, claim that making love during menstruation does not bother them. Others find that the increased dampness caused by the blood reduces their sensations. This often belies a certain repulsion. Most often, however, it is women themselves who refuse to have intercourse during their periods. They are afraid of staining the bed sheets or, at least subconsciously, of 'sullying' their partner.

Do large penises necessarily give more pleasure to women?

The length of the penis contributes little to female pleasure as the vaginal erogenous zones are less than two inches from the vulva. Furthermore, sexologists have noted that women are often afraid that overly imposing members will make intercourse painful.

Despite the increasingly open attitude of the media towards the subject of menstruation (for example the increased frequency of television commercials on new, improved feminine-hygiene products supposedly enabling women to carry on with their lives as usual), menstruation continues to provoke deep-rooted fears that modernity has not completely succeeded in overcoming. Primitive men believed menstruation endowed women with supernatural powers, enabling them to command storms and lightning simply by walking around naked. The lost blood was believed to have magical properties, and so was painted on warriors' bodies during battle to protect them from injury. Small quantities of menstrual blood were believed to be capable of extinguishing fires. In the Middle Ages, menstrual blood was stripped of its magical powers and became associated instead with demonic practice. Menstruating women were not permitted to take communion, and in some cases were refused entry into churches. Some religious cultures, such as orthodox Jews, absolutely forbid sexual intercourse during menstruation; historically, it was believed that there was something unhealthy or unholy about menstrual blood.

Such beliefs may no longer be at all widely held, but echoes of them remain, even if only in the chambers of the unconscious mind. For example, some mothers still advise their daughters to avoid swimming, showering, or bathing during menstruation. This is absurd. Menstruation is as natural a physiological function as digestion, and menstruating women should not be subjected to any restrictions except those concerning basic personal hygiene and sexual choices.

◆ *What different methods of contraception are available?*

Pregnancy is the result of three successive stages: the ovary lays an ovule; the ovule is fertilized inside the fallopian tubes, and the fertilized egg attaches itself to the wall of the uterus. Pregnancy can be prevented at several stages in this process. The combined pill blocks ovulation by switching off the ovaries; progestogen-only pills can block ovulation, but also have an effect on the lining of the uterus and the cervical mucus. Progestogens can also be given in the form of injectables or implants to prevent pregnancy and are very effective methods. There is also an emergency pill that must be taken within 72 hours of intercourse. It can prevent ovulation if given in the early part of the cycle and it also modifies the lining of the uterus, making it inhospitable to the nesting egg. The RU486, which was developed by Professor Etienne Baulieu, exercises an abortive action by blocking the hormone necessary for the maintenance of the pregnancy. An emergency IUD can be fitted as well; this is fitted within five days of intercourse, or up to day 19 of a woman with a 28-day cycle. Like an ordinary IUD (see page 121), it prevents the egg from nesting by modifying the mucous membrane of the uterus. IUDs have been used for many decades to prevent conception; modern IUDs are very effective and can last for five years or more. A recent innovation is a hormone-releasing intra-uterine system, which has been proved to be very effective and can diminish menstruation.

Condoms, diaphragms, vaginal suppositories, and spermicidal jellies are mechanical or chemical methods used locally to prevent spermatozoa from entering the uterine cavity. The female condom, which was developed recently in response to the threat of AIDS, provides a solution to the problem of men who refuse to wear condoms. It consists of a polyurethane latex envelope that lines the vaginal walls and protects the cervix. However, some couples have difficulty in manipulating and positioning the female condom.

Surgical contraceptive methods – tubal ligation for women and vasectomies for men – are also available. In the first case, the fallopian tubes are tied or clipped to prevent the ovule from passing through and being fertilized by a sperm. The ovaries and uterus remain intact, and menstruation continues. In principle, this is an effective method with almost a zero failure rate. However, women considering this method must give it very serious thought, as they may change their minds and wish to have a baby; in such a situation, surgery will be required to untie the tubes. This method is rarely carried out on women without children and is usually used when pregnancy threatens a woman's health and/or life.

A vasectomy involves obstructing the trajectory of the deferent channels which connect the testicles with the urethra; and through which the spermatozoa flow. Sexual functioning remains unchanged by the operation, and neither erection nor ejaculation are inhibited. But men must wait two to three months for the spermatozoa that remain upstream of the knot to die before they can enjoy the benefits of the operation. It is difficult to reverse this operation, although spontaneous re-generation has been know to occur. For this reason, spermograms (examination of sperm under a microscope) are generally prescribed three months after the operation to ensure that no spermatozoa are present. Because the operation is not easily reversible, men who are considering vasectomies should think seriously before consenting to the operation.

Does the pill have any side-effects?

The pill has been greatly improved since its introduction in the 1960s. However, some women may find they gain weight when they take the pill, and there are some women who should not use this form of contraception for health reasons.

The pill

The pill used today is very different from those used in the 1960s. The required dosage is lower, and it is made from synthetic hormones that are closer to natural hormones. As a result, the pill is more easily tolerated by the body. The pill works like this: ovulation is blocked when estrogen and progesterone, which are synthetic hormones, 'mime' the natural secretion of the ovaries, resulting in an artificial hormonal cycle as well as in modification of the uterine mucous membrane and cervical mucus.

There are two types of pill available: combined pills and progestogen-only pills. Combined pills contain estrogen and progestin; there are several kinds available, with different types and quantities of hormones. Progestogen-only pills only contain progestin; they may be more suitable for older women or women who are not able to tolerate estrogens.

How to use the pill: Combined pills should be taken every day, at approximately the same time of day, beginning on the first day of menstruation. When the pack is finished, menstruation occurs. A new pack is started after seven days of not taking the pill, even if the period has not yet ended. Progestogen-only pills are taken every day with no breaks and should be taken at the same time each day.

Advantages: The pill is an effective method of contraception – providing you do not forget to take it. Also, some women experience reduced menstrual pain when they are on the pill.

Disadvantages: Women who are at an increased risk from cardiovascular problems, thrombosis, or stroke, such as smokers or women who have problems with weight, hypertension, or high cholesterol levels, may be advised not to take the pill. Caution may also be necessary in women with a history of certain types of cancer.

Do IUDs have to be replaced regularly?

There are two types of IUD: hormone-releasing IUDs, which must be replaced every three years, and copper IUDs, which should be replaced every five years, and some types can last even longer. The procedure should be carried out by a physician.

IUDs

This inch-long device prevents implantation of the egg by causing a slight, permanent inflammation of the uterine mucous membrane. There are two types of IUD: copper IUDs have copper wire wound round the stem of the coil; hormone-releasing IUDs have a reservoir containing progestin attached to the stem. This has the additional effect of obstructing the progression of spermatozoa. The IUD is inserted by a doctor, preferably immediately after menstruation to eliminate any risk that the woman is already pregnant.

Advantages: The IUD method does not change the hormonal cycle.

Disadvantages: Menstruation may be heavier with copper IUDs, but hormone-releasing IUDs can markedly diminish menstrual loss. Copper IUDs will not prevent pelvic inflammatory disease, especially if the woman is at risk of acquiring an STD.

Diaphragms and spermicides

Diaphragms and spermicides work together to mechanically and chemically prevent contact between the ovule and the spermatozoa. Spermicidal products are not very reliable if used on their own and should always be used in conjunction with another method.

The correct size of a diaphragm should be determined by a physician. It is covered with spermicidal cream and inserted into the vagina to cover the cervix. It can be inserted up to three hours before intercourse and should not be removed for at least six hours afterwards. (Your doctor will ensure the diaphragm is the correct size for your body.) If intercourse takes place again before the diaphragm has been removed, then more spermicide should be added with the help of an applicator. The diaphragm should be left in place for another six hours.

Advantages: Immediate use with no risks. It can help to protect the cervix from cervical cancer and can also help prevent pelvic inflammatory disease.

Disadvantages: No baths or douching for six hours following intercourse. Use of diaphragms and spermicides can also sometimes cause temporary irritation.

Condoms

The condom is the only contraceptive method that also protects against sexually-transmitted diseases. Condoms prevent the sperm from penetrating the vagina. When new partners begin having sex, the man should always wear a condom to protect against STDs generally, and the AIDS virus specifically.

The condom should be placed on the erect penis before penetration, as a small amount of seminal fluid containing sperm leaks out during intercourse even if ejaculation does not occur.

It is best to use condoms with a small pouch at the tip. If there is is no pouch, pinch the latex to make some extra room. Some condoms are lubricated; for those that are not, additional lubrication can be used, but not oil-based lubricants as these can damage the condom. The man must withdraw from the vagina immediately after ejaculation, holding the condom at the base to prevent it remaining in the vagina.

Advantages: Condoms present no health risks outside of several, rare allergies to latex.

Disadvantages: Use of the condom requires full erection. They must be put on carefully (pay attention to sharp nails, which can tear the latex), as they are fragile and can break at a critical moment. If a condom does break, the man should advise his partner to seek emergency contraception to prevent an unplanned pregnancy.

Most 'natural' methods of contraception are risky.

The Ogino or calendar method was popular in the days before the pill was invented. *It is unreliable as a method of contraception, as are the temperature and Billing's methods.*

The 'natural' methods

Natural methods of contraception involve abstaining from sexual intercourse during the fertile time in a woman's cycle. They are most commonly used by some religious groups such as Catholics, who do not believe in other methods of family planning. There are three ways to determine a woman's fertile time: the Ogino or calendar method, the temperature method, and the Billing's method.

The Ogino or calendar method: This involves working out the fertile time each month based on the previous six to twelve cycles. A woman with a 28-day cycle will need to avoid intercourse between days 8 and 18.

The temperature method: The woman takes her temperature each morning before getting up. A temperature rise of 0.36–0.72°F indicates the start of ovulation. Sexual relations are resumed on the third day after this increase, and can continue until menstruation begins.

The Billing's method: Vaginal secretions indicate when ovulation begins. The mucus becomes abundant and clear, resembling the white of an egg. Intercourse should stop until the third day after this change.

How 'natural' methods work: By avoiding intercourse during fertile periods in the cycle pregnancy should not occur.

Advantages: No harmful side effects.

Disadvantages: The Ogino method is rarely used today, as it has an approximately 40 percent failure rate, especially at the extremes of the reproductive years when menstruation tends to be less regular. The temperature method is unreliable if the woman has to be up at night, either working or taking care of a baby. This disrupts her temperature curve. Finally, difficulties in the Billing's method arise from uncertainties in determining the change in the mucus. Women also dislike its overtly 'clinical' aspect.

How can I control my excitement during lovemaking? Do lovemaking techniques really exist? Can women have multiple orgasms? Is it usual to have erotic fantasies, and can they be acted out? Sexuality is something everyone is curious about, and there are answers to all these questions. But we should still try to keep a bit of the mystery.

◆ Why do some people scream when they are making love?

Screaming, crying, sighing, and moaning – the list is not exhaustive – are emotional responses. They are psychosomatic reactions to existential moments of deep meaning (such as love-making) for the individual. Emotions, and more specifically, erotic cries constitute a sort of 'metalanguage' that communicates a person's intense pleasure to his or her partner. There is nothing more titillating than hearing your partner express pleasure at the full capacity of his or her lungs. Screaming, crying, and groaning also help people to release erotic tensions and paroxysms.

◆ How long should sexual intercourse last?

The idea that there is a 'normal' length of time for lovemaking stems from either pure arbitrariness, obsessional neuroses, or the aberrant and dictatorial impulses of a politico-amorous regimen. The 'appropriate' length of time for intercourse is a matter for lovers themselves to decide, but one can 'reasonably' expect that intercourse lasting less than five minutes will lead to frustration and that, conversely, lovemaking for over ten hours straight will reduce the participants to a state of jelly. Statistics indicate that the average length of time for intercourse is between ten and

How long, on average, does it take to reach climax?

Men generally climax much more quickly than women. Statistics show that, on average, men reach orgasm in less than four minutes, whereas women take at least twice as long. It is therefore important for partners to find ways of allowing for these differences.

twelve minutes for males and between eight and ten minutes for females. These figures, however, do not constitute a norm.

It is important to recognize that there is a difference between male and female arousal curves. Men usually reach orgasm in less than four minutes, and women in eight.

The role of foreplay is, therefore, important in harmonizing the different intensities of desire between men and women. The duration of lovemaking is entirely subjective. In short, there is only one timepiece, and that is what is dictated by the heart and the senses. As Shakespeare wrote, 'Love alters not, with his brief hours and weeks.'

◆ What causes nocturnal and morning erections?

Nocturnal erections occur during the dream phase of the REM sleep cycle. The sleeper's penis stiffens, his eyeballs move about rapidly beneath the lids, and the small muscles of his fingers and toes contract as if he were actively participating in his own dreams.

Morning erection occurs during the last phase of REM sleep, especially when the bladder is full and applying pressure to the prostate. Stimulation of the prostate leads to erection. In cases where it is difficult to determine whether impotence arises from physiological or mental causes, the continued occurrence of morning erections – which are purely physiological – indicates that the impotence has psychological causes.

Puberty usually starts between the ages of ten and 14. One of the first signs of maturity is the occurrence of the first erection and ejaculation. This often happens at night, as a so-called wet dream. Men are more likely to have nocturnal erections and emissions if they are not sexually active and do not masturbate.

Is it necessary to control one's desire?

The answer is 'yes'. Foreplay will increase your sexual appetite, and it relaxes women, helping to banish inhibitions and so enabling them fully to enjoy themselves. So, take your time and control your desire - it will be worth it.

◆ Do sexual techniques exist?

The term 'sexual techniques' is unfortunate in that it evokes images of rules, norms, and methods. Most people pick up ideas about sexual practices from their older brothers and sisters, from books and movies, or from their own experiences, but none of these are surefire methods; there is no single bag of tricks guaranteed to please every partner. The best 'technique' in lovemaking is to desire your partner. Desire sharpens the senses and encourages the imagination. It empowers lovers' sixth sense for finding the caresses and words that will open the gates to pleasure.

For most women, their sensuality is first awakened mentally; immediate genital stimulation is too functional and mechanical, inhibiting them from abandoning themselves to sexual pleasure. Even during 'one night stands,' there is a positive interaction between love and sexuality. For something to be worthwhile usually requires a bit of effort and this also applies to the achievement of sexual well-being. Knowledge of how your body and your partner's body work, how they respond to different types of stimulation, and the ability to use that knowledge will be very rewarding. All the senses – sight, smell, sound, and touch – are involved in providing pleasure.

The pressure of a hand and the exchange of meaningful looks can be erotically charged. Relationships between partners vary, but kindness, courtesy, and awareness of the other person's state of arousal are all indispensable ingredients of any successful sexual encounter. Lovemaking is fueled by the overtures and the complex nuances of verbal caresses. Take your time in bed, share fantasies, play games, and try different positions. Rushing through the act of love is as much a waste as spending all day in your hotel on your first visit to a great city!

◆ How can I control my excitement during lovemaking?

We have seen how essential foreplay is to good sexual relations. But both partners should be constantly aware of each other's level of arousal, as extended foreplay may cause one of the partners to reach a climax too soon. During penetration, the woman can slow down the momentum and check her partner's excitement by controlling the movement of her pelvis and intravaginal contractions. If the man feels that he is losing control and about to come, he can delay orgasm by pulling out for several seconds until his sensations subside a little. When the woman is on top, she can adjust the movements of penetration to suit her partner's state of arousal; this is particularly useful with men who are prone to premature ejaculation. Squeezing the base of the penis is another good way of delaying orgasm. Most importantly, abdominal breathing, which has the effect of reactivating the parasympathetic nervous system, enables the man to delay ejaculation without stopping or slowing down coital movements.

◆ Does the art of pleasure exist?

Since time immemorial, man has attempted to attain full self-consciousness in two ways: through religion (etymologically derived from the Latin verb *religare*, meaning to connect), and through eroticism (Eros was the Greek god of erotic love, who showered life with arrows steeped in the magic potion of love). Religion glorifies the spirit, and eroticism sanctifies the body.

Hindus decorate their temples with scenes of surprisingly realistic and sophisticated couplings. The strangest and most awkward positions imaginable are depicted in paintings

What are the techniques for delaying orgasm?

When the man feels that he is about to come, he can withdraw for a few seconds. Squeezing the base of the penis is another effective method of delaying orgasm. When the woman is on top, she can adjust her rate of movement to control her partner's state of arousal.

and sculptures. With the thousands of recipes for lovemaking assembled by Vatsyayana in the *Kama Sutra*, games of the body acquired a new status. No longer merely ways to ease or assuage the senses, these practices emerged as a celebrated art form which, though not unique (from as far back as the early Stone Age, sculptors have produced women with heavy breasts and prominent and open vulvas) is richly diverse, educating, and life-affirming. Ovid, meanwhile, wrote *The Art of Love* and Plato celebrated a new art of loving, more cerebral than erotic, that kindled the passions through modesty and reserve, titillating the senses through abstinence and the flurry of exchanged glances, rather than through the intertwining of bodies.

Art is inseparable from pleasure and the sublime; through literature, painting, and sculpture, the passions are ennobled, pleasure is nourished, and desire is turned away from monotony and set free to discover all the secrets paths of the soul.

◆ How do women reach orgasm?

Female orgasms are generally more difficult to achieve than male orgasms. Three factors seem to account for this: excitement must be maintained at a certain level over a relatively long period, which is only possible when the woman is mentally uninhibited; women are much more sensitive to distractions such as noise, bad breath, or the presence of a third person; and finally, despite today's more liberal social mores, a sociocultural history of sexual repression is more deeply ingrained in women than in men. Clitoral stimulation during foreplay is important in bringing a woman to orgasm. When the clitoris is unaroused or, as in the case of certain African and Egyptian women, absent, the man must increase his

movements, sometimes violently, but with invariably inefficient results. Orgasms trigger a reflex wave between the sense-receptive zone of the clitoris and the area controlling the movements of the perivaginal muscles. They are produced by the simultaneous action of the numerous nerve endings which surround the clitoris and intervaginal contractions.

◆ Can prolonged intercourse be harmful?

Subjective factors such as desire, fatigue, and age make it difficult to determine what constitutes excessively prolonged intercourse. But extended intercourse generally decreases the natural lubrication of vaginal secretions, making penetration painful. A 'dry' vagina can also be painful for men.

◆ Does prolonged erection always end in ejaculation?

Erection, even when prolonged, does not inevitably end in ejaculation for several reasons, the most common being age and, consequently, diminished performance. Although the man is able to maintain an erection, he is not sufficiently aroused for ejaculation. This also occurs in young men.

This is often a physiological response to anxiety or an uncontrolled emotion. It may originate from an initial sexual encounter with an extremely desirable woman, toward whom, nonetheless, the man harbored unconscious hostility. This type of problem occurs in isolated incidents and does not follow any discernible pattern. But some men suffer from inhibited ejaculation, the term used to describe the inability to ejaculate, which is a symptom of a partial or total psychological problem. Men suffering from inhibited ejaculation can only ejaculate during wet dreams. This is because,

What are the causes of difficulties in 'getting it up'?

Men find this problem very embarrassing, but most suffer from it at some time or other. Occasional difficulty in gaining an erection should not be a source of worry: the man may simply be tired, or have drunk too much. In more serious cases (where a man has repeated problems in gaining and maintaining an erection), some 40 percent are, in general, attributable to psychological causes, 30 percent are attributable to physiological causes, and 30 percent to a mixture of the two.

while sleeping, their inhibitions and self-censorship are suspended. Generally speaking, inhibited ejaculation is selective and does not occur consistently.

A person suffering from this condition can still ejaculate when masturbating or during fleeting sexual relations with, for instance, a prostitute or homosexual. On the other hand, he will be incapable of ejaculating when having sexual relations with his wife. The problem may be symptomatic of a conscious rejection of the wife or, in some cases, a refusal to have a child. It may also be a feeling of insecurity associated with the fear of abandonment. It is a way of punishing the partner.

Some men also suffer from retrograde-ejaculation in which the sperm goes back into the bladder. This is sometimes caused by abnormalities in the ejaculating channels and the urethra. It occurs most frequently after prostate surgery.

◆ How does a woman know when she has had an orgasm?

Heavy breathing, the loss of strong feelings, waves of pleasure sweeping all thoughts and ideas aside, and intense vaginal contractions even after the penis has been withdrawn – these are only some of the signs of orgasm. Orgasms cannot be defined in any one way as they differ greatly from one person to the next. Some women exteriorize their pleasure by screaming, others silently focus on their sensations.

Studies of orgasms reveal that the term 'ecstatic' recurs most frequently when women try to describe their emotions, indicating a close relationship between mystical exaltation and sexually orgasmic feelings. The whole body can be involved, with spasmodic contractions of the limbs, fingers, toes, and face.

◆ Can women have multiple orgasms?

Unlike men, who become sleepy, and whose penis grows soft after ejaculation, women can have several orgasms during intercourse. But one should not make the mistake of assuming that all women have multiple orgasms. Many women, like their partners, feel so satiated and relaxed after a single orgasm that it becomes impossible to bring her to another climax.

◆ Is it normal to have erotic fantasies?

Fantasies are a normal part of sexual relationships. They allow us to enact in our minds the sadomasochistic drives that exist within all of us. Fantasies are outlets for unfulfilled desires; they allow us to step out of our everyday selves and turn the tables on reality. For example a shy, gullible, man, who is preyed upon by circumstances and the people around him, may fantasize about being a tough guy with many girlfriends.

Fetishism and compensatory desires also express themselves through fantasy. The timid wife who is completely faithful to her husband may imagine having frenzied sex with the quiet and serious-looking neighbor from downstairs. Or, perhaps, with the thug who lives across the street, an arrogant young man who stares knowingly at her every time they meet outside. Fantasies are as rich and varied as human nature itself, and the only limits on them are the limitations of the imagination itself.

Some fantasies seem to belong to a sort of 'collective imagination,' that is shared by most people. They arise from social and cultural taboos that set limits to sexuality according to the rules and mores of the time. Fantasies also stem from each person's different emotional or sexual needs. Essentially, fantasies about rape, incest, and orgies fit into this pattern.

Are women sexually insatiable?

This is of course a fantasy, but one that nonetheless contains a germ of fact. For a woman's physiology does indeed allow her to experience multiple orgasms – something that a man is generally unable to do. Because of this, women sometimes experience acute sexual frustration, a problem that a partner is often unable fully to appreciate.

A man who feels insecure about the size of his penis will fantasize about deflowering his cousin with his huge 10-inch member. A woman who is bored by sex with her husband will imagine being raped by the plumber. Another woman who is sexually dissatisfied but too faithful to her husband to take a lover fantasizes that she is the most beautiful flower in a succulent harem of women. She is at the mercy of her master's whims and is forced to satisfy the lust of his guests.

◆ Should fantasies be acted out?

It seems clear that few people would want to experience their secret fantasies in real life. Erotic literature and films such as *The Philosophy in the Boudoir* by Sade, *Venus in Furs* by Sacher-Masoch, *The Story of O*, and *Emmanuelle*, which have fed the fantasies of so many readers and moviegoers, are themselves the products of their authors' fantasies. The Marquis de Sade, for example, who spent most of his life in an asylum, was imprisoned not for his sexual practices but for his writing.

In attempting to turn fantasy into real life, one runs the risk of committing reprehensible acts that are legally prohibited. There is also the possibility of disappointment when a fantasy that was so vivid and colorful in the imagination turns out to be sadly mediocre once acted out. Nevertheless, when two consenting adults decide to act out a fantasy, this can be a source of intense satisfaction.

Generally, most people fantasize during masturbation and intercourse. This is very healthy, as desire begins in your head and finds expression through fantasy. When fantasies become boring, all you have to do is change them. Acting out fantasies sometimes takes away their erotic power since they lose their status as 'forbidden fruit.'

◆ How should I feel about my sexual fantasies?

Your fantasies reflect the way in which your sexuality has evolved since infancy. This includes the incestuous or oedipal desires that we have all felt and repressed for social and moral reasons. Fantasies may sometimes be vestiges of a real-life erotic scene that occurred during childhood with an adult.

Fantasies are outlets for the libido to liberate and ease itself without transgressing certain laws. Fantasy replenishes desire and enriches sexual relations while also allowing us to deal with frustrations when we find ourselves alone and unfulfilled.

◆ Should a couple make love every day?

Any attitude expressed by 'should' flies in the face of a sexual relationship built on desire. Desire itself is already dependent on so many factors, such as physical and mental well-being, a harmonious, loving relationship, and the absence of conflict. Statistics show that sexual activity decreases regularly with time. Frequency of sexual intercourse is always greatest at the start of a new relationship, but in the majority of long-term relationships it will occur about one or two times a week. The most intense sexual activity has been observed to occur between the ages of 30 and 40.

For a woman, the frequency of sexual intercourse is less connected to her capacity for orgasm than to her narcissistic needs. Constant admiration and reassurance from her partner will make her feel seductive and beautiful. The quality of the union is more important to the woman than the quantity of sex that is involved in the relationship.

Sexual rapport relies on harmony between the heart, body, and the mind.

Where do fantasies originate?

Humans have an innate capacity both to give and to receive pain; hence the frequency of sadomasochistic fantasies. Generally, though, fantasies act as a safe way of releasing dissatisfaction or frustration, which are often themselves caused by the taboos that society places on certain forms of sexual activity.

◆ Can pregnant women make love?

Popular belief still holds that pregnant women must forego sexual activity to avoid traumatizing the fetus and risking abortion. In fact, there is no need for abstinence so long as positions are chosen that are comfortable for the mother-to-be. During the first trimester, many women experience a drop in sexual desire. This may be caused by her state of health: nausea, vomiting, fatigue, sleepiness, and muscular pain, as well as fear of hurting the fetus.

During the second trimester, however, most women are sexually voracious. There are several positions that are comfortable for both partners, and that prevent the man from feeling 'crushed' by his partner's belly. The woman can get on top or both partners can lie side by side.

During the last trimester, fatigue and a tendency to breathlessness cause a decrease in sexual activity. In some cases, the doctor who is monitoring the pregnancy will advise the woman to limit or stop all intercourse. However, this is not necessarily true for all cases, and if there are no specific risks or problems, sexual relations can continue up until delivery.

Nonetheless, for women who suffer from an 'irritated' uterus, which carries some risk of abortion, intercourse may cause uterine contractions that may be harmful.

It is up to the doctor to gauge the situation. But it is important to remember that if all sexual activity stops during pregnancy, the future father may resort to satisfying himself elsewhere.

Some women experience their first orgasm during pregnancy as the idea of maternity is strongly connected to pleasure. Couples may find it helpful to explore different positions, especially during the last trimester.

Do we all have the same sexual fantasies?

Certain fantasies seem to spring from a 'collective unconscious' – we all seem to experience them to a greater or lesser degree. The most common are to do with rape, incest, or being in a harem. Such fantasies act as a safety valve, allowing us to imagine situations which are taboo, and which we would not, in any case, wish to act out in real life.

◆ How long after giving birth should women wait before resuming sexual relations?

If the mother does not breast-feed, menstruation usually begins again six to eight weeks after giving birth. If she does breast-feed, the length of time can stretch out to three months. She can begin taking the pill again from one to 15 days after delivery, provided that she is not breast-feeding. This way, she can resume sexual activity before her periods start again without having to worry about getting pregnant.

◆ What effect does alcohol have on sexual activity?

Alcohol is probably the most widely used drug in the Western world. In small quantities, it can act as an aphrodisiac, resulting in a pleasant, feeling of warmth and relaxing a person's sexual anxieties. Ethanol, which is the active substance in alcohol, has psychotropic properties. It is antidepressive, anxiolytic, and psychotonic, and reduces inhibitions. These have different repercussions depending on the individual. Psychotonic properties, or ones that reduce inhibitions, may make men believe that they are more virile. A little alcohol is sufficient to reduce mental inhibitions by increasing the rate of excitement. Individuals vary in their response to alcohol and will experience different effects depending on the amount of alcohol consumed and the chronicity of its use. If individuals consume greater amounts of alcohol, they may become drowsy and find that sensitivity is impaired. This can result in an inability to get or maintain an erection in men and loss of orgasmic ability in women. Larger quantities of alcohol can also result in loss of self-restraint, which may in turn lead to violence and sexual assault.

◆ What causes sexual incompatibility?

It is difficult to pinpoint the reasons why some couples have good sexual rapport and others do not. Conflicting moral values, the fear of failure or abandonment, and the inability to abandon oneself to erotic sensations are only some of the things that contribute to misunderstanding. Esthetic criteria, whether conscious or unconscious, are linked to what Carl Jung referred to as the 'imagos' – unconscious representations of family members. These carry powerful emotional weight. They affect our interpersonal relationships, orient our sympathies and expectations, and command our antipathies and aversions in friendship, love, and desire.

We often forget how important our sense of smell is in sexual attraction. The physiological explanation for this lies in the primitive brain, that reptiles and lower mammals still possess. Vestiges of this primitive brain are found in humans; it is linked to the sense of smell and harbors the centers of sexual pleasure and aggression.

◆ What is vaginismus?

Vaginismus is an involuntary tightening of the vaginal muscles; some women get so tense about the thought of having sexual intercourse that their vaginal muscles contract, and penetration by the man's penis then becomes very painful and sometimes impossible. Vaginismus can be primary, occuring the first time that intercourse is attempted, or secondary, when intercourse has previously taken place and is now impossible. Primary vaginismus usually occurs in young women; they may have fears that intercourse will be very painful the first time, or that the vagina will not be big enough to take the penis; or it

Which is the best position when making love to a pregnant woman?

To prevent the woman from over-exerting herself, or being squashed by the weight of her partner, two positions are ideal: the woman can get on top (where she can control the pace of lovemaking), or the partners can lie side-by-side, spoon-fashion.

could occur as a result of the fear of pregnancy. Worries about the act of intercourse will also stop the normal vaginal secretions that occur when a woman becomes excited; this will result in a dry vagina, which will make penetration uncomfortable and aggravate vaginismus. In extreme cases, vaginismus will lead to nonconsummation of the relationship. Secondary vaginismus may occur following infections of the vagina, after vaginal injury or ulceration, or in the postmenopause, when the vagina may shrink and become very dry.

Women who experience vaginismus will be advised to try relaxation techniques prior to intercourse. An emphasis on foreplay before penetration will enable the woman to become more excited and her vaginal secretions will then start to flow, but sometimes it may be helpful to use a lubricant. Women can be shown how to use vaginal dilators in different sizes, starting with the smallest and progressing to larger ones. This should help to allay any fears about the size of her vagina. Occasionally, women may have to seek help from a psychotherapist or psychosexual counselor.

◆ Is it normal to masturbate?

The one form of sex that is absolutely safe, because you cannot get pregnant or contract a sexually transmitted disease, is self-masturbation. Infants and young children quite commonly handle and play with their genitals; it is normal for them to do so and helps them to discover their own bodies and the physical differences between the sexes. They should not be made to feel ashamed about this behavior or that it is wrong, as it may lead them to be sexually inhibited or to have sexual problems later in life. As a result of the hormone changes in puberty, adolescents have an increased urge to masturbate. Studies have shown that nearly all boys have masturbated to orgasm by the age of 18. For girls, masturbation may be a way to defer sexual intercourse. Masturbation continues throughout life; it occurs at all ages, amongst the married and unmarried, and in the elderly. It is useful as a means of relieving sexual tension if one lacks a partner and can also be an aid in happy and loving relationships especially if one partner is stressed.

◆ Can a woman get pregnant if she doesn't have an orgasm?

It is a myth that a woman cannot get pregnant if she doesn't have an orgasm. It is true that when a woman has an orgasm, the vaginal contractions that occur cause the cervix to dip into the pool of ejaculate at the bottom of the vagina and therefore make it easier for the sperm to swim up into the uterus through the cervix. However, some of the sperm will make their way through the cervix anyway and pregnancy can result whether the woman has multiple orgasms or none at all.

◆ What is the G-spot?

The G-spot was named after Dr. Ernst Grafenburg, a German obstetrician and gynecologist. Forty years ago he claimed to have found a spot in the vagina that could give women orgasms without clitoral stimulation. Stimulation of the G-spot reputedly produces intense excitement, and the resultant orgasm is said to be much stronger than a clitoral orgasm. The G-spot is supposed to be located on the front wall of the vagina, and some people believe that it is a rudimentary prostate gland situated around the urethra, although pathologists have failed to locate it in the course of post-mortems.

To drink, or to make love: do we have to choose?

Drinking a small amount of alcohol will make us feel more relaxed and less inhibited – in short, feel more sexy. Drinking too much alcohol, though, damages sexual performance. For example, we'll feel less energetic (even sleepy), the senses will become dulled, and men may have difficulty in getting an erection.

Questions and Answers – Sex After Sixty

*D*oes sexual appetite always decrease as we grow older? Do prostate operations lead to impotence? Does male menopause exist, and up to what age do men remain fertile? Growing old brings many questions and much anxiety, especially since sexuality is strongly associated with youth. But isn't there a saying that old pots produce the best soup?

◆ Does sexual desire diminish with age?

Age brings about many physical changes: we tire more quickly after physical exertion, our sleep requirements are altered, and our body undergoes a variety of functional changes. Nonetheless, in matters of love, the brain remains the primary sexual organ. The psychological impact of menopause is an important factor in determining whether or not a woman continues to have sex. Many men also think that menopause signals the end of sexual activity, but they are confusing procreation with eroticism. According to the Kinsey* report, there is a correlation between sexual activity at an advanced age and how early a woman began having sexual relations. For elderly people, sex rejuvenates both the body and the mind.

* Alfred Charles Kinsey (1894–1956), an American biologist, conducted research on sexual matters such as intercourse, masturbation, fantasies, and perversions for the University of Indiana and the Rockefeller Foundation. During the course of his research, he interviewed 16,000 people from all over the United States. His conclusions showed that existing sexual practices contradicted the mores of that time (partner exchanges, sodomy, fetishism), proving that sexual desire defies all social and legal prohibitions.

The end of periods - the beginning of the end?

In the minds of many, the end of menstruation, marking as it does the start of the menopause, also signals the end of a healthy sex life. But there is no reason why sexual relations between partners should cease.

◆ Up to what age do men remain fertile?

From an endocrinological point of view, the hormone level begins to decline after the age of 50. But for most men, hormonal and genital changes do not necessarily affect sexuality. Although the change in secretions diminishes sexual activity in the long run, this happens very gradually. Therefore, there is no fixed age after which procreation becomes impossible. While it is true that, with time, sperm become less mobile and decrease in quantity, these changes vary for each individual.

◆ Do prostate operations lead to impotence?

From age 50 onward, the prostate may undergo fiber degeneration, or prostatic adenoma may develop (the latter is usually caused by a hormonal imbalance). This type of adenoma causes the urethra to be compressed which, in turn, obstructs urination, sometimes resulting in complete urine retention in the bladder. Surgery may be necessary to regain sexual potency. Operations of this kind have two possible consequences: the volume of seminal liquid decreases and some men experience retrograde-ejaculation. Although this is not dangerous, it can diminish orgasmic sensation.

Mental factors also play an important role in maintaining sexual activity. A man may feel devalued and less sure of himself, and see the surgery as morally and psychologically castrating. This may eventually lead to secondary impotence, which can be overcome with good medical counseling both before and after the operation. Prostate cancer is usually treated by surgical removal or radiation. Sometimes it may be treated by hormones which may result in a loss of libido or difficulty in getting and keeping an erection.

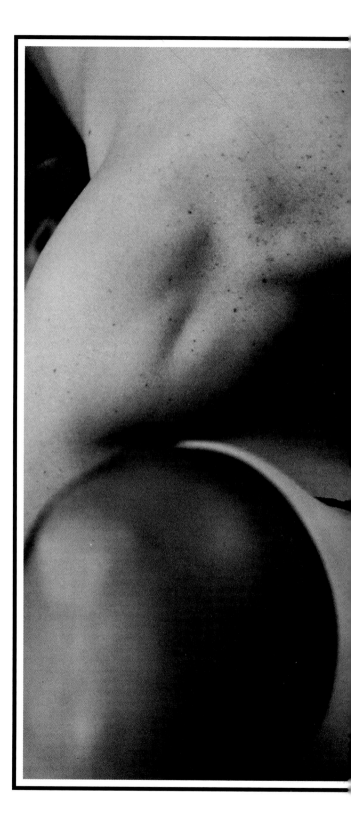

Is is possible to father a child at the age of 60?

With increased life expectancy, the sight of happy new fathers who happen to be of retirement age is becoming more common. Scientifically, there is no reason why a man of 60 should not father children, as sperm production continues indefinitely in men.

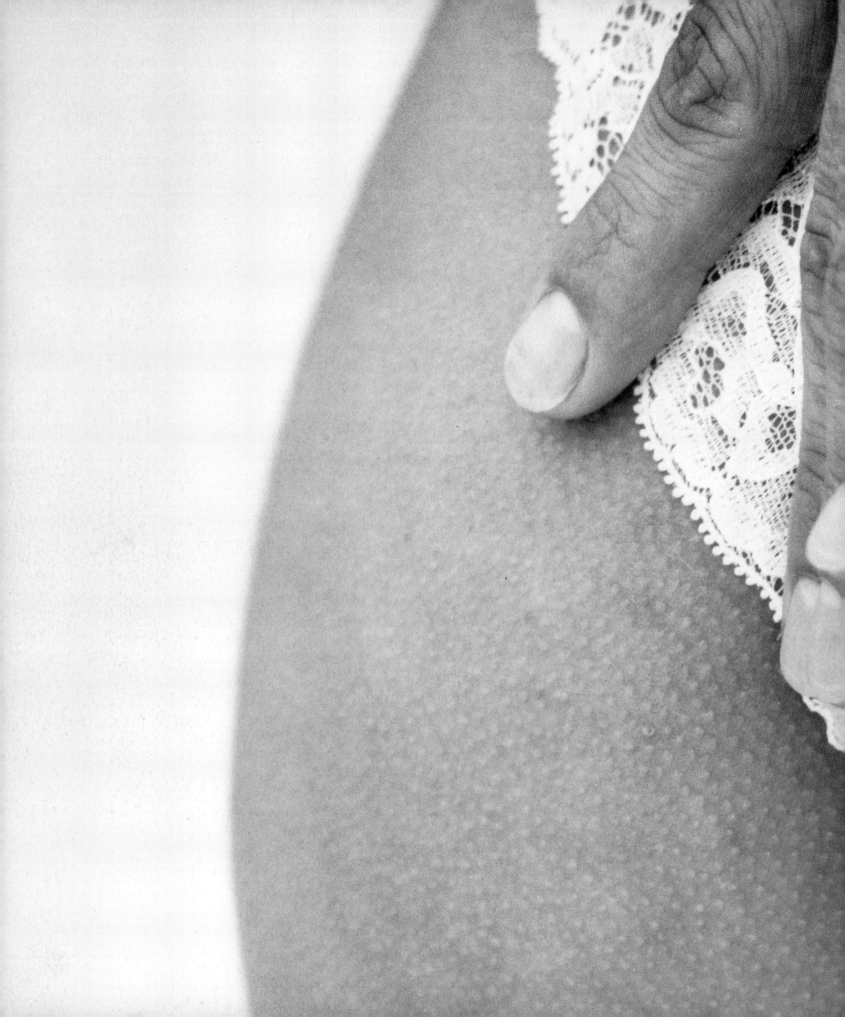

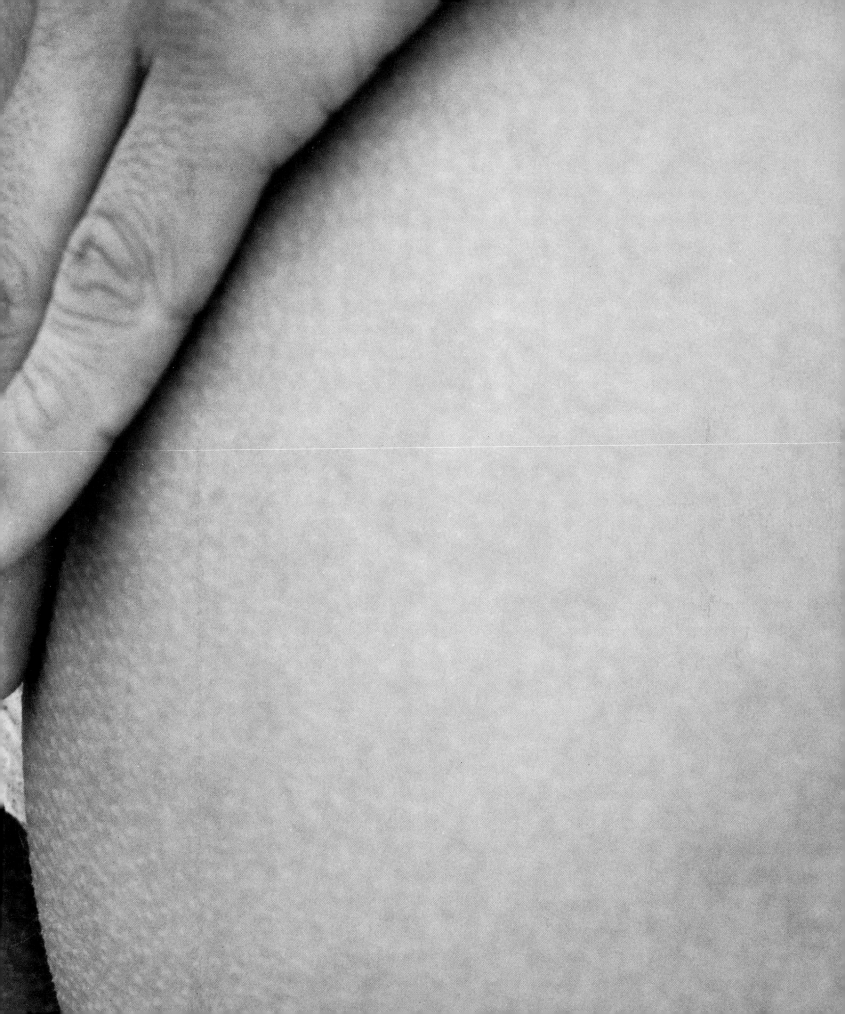

◆ What is menopause?

Menopause occurs when the ovaries grow old, causing menstruation and reproductive functions to cease. For a number of reasons, such as the biological programming established at birth, or rapid aging due to a hostile environment, the ovary is no longer able to ovulate. Physiological aging occurs in two separate phases: the first is the premenopausal phase, in which menstrual cycles alternate with nonmenstrual cycles, depending on whether or not an ovum has been produced; the second – the menopausal phase itself – occurs several months or even years after ovulation has stopped completely.

Only humans experience the termination of reproduction. Monkeys and dogs, for example, can give birth until they are extremely old, whereas women lose this capacity between 45 and 55 years of age, and sometimes at the age of 35. Unlike animal offspring, who become independent from their mothers early on, the human child is dependent on the mother until the age of 10. What is more, women who become pregnant after the age of 40 run a higher risk of producing chromosomal anomalies in the fetus. However these anomalies can be detected, early in the pregnancy, through amniocentesis.

Menopause therefore serves, in effect, to aid in the selection and preservation of the species. Menopause is accompanied by physical as well as mental symptoms, such as hot flushes, vaginal dryness, and nervousness. These symptoms are easily eliminated by means of hormone-substitute treatments. Most importantly, menopause is associated with the idea of the end of sexual activity, as many people confuse procreation with femininity. In fact, this may be a period of sexual 'fertility,' as the woman no longer has to worry about pregnancy and contraception, and her experience and maturity should, in principle, allow her to overcome the many fears and taboos that affect the quality of pleasure for younger women.

Is the menopause just something dreamt up by doctors?

The answer is 'No,' as there are clearly a number of physical symptoms of menopause: 'hot flushes,' vaginal dryness, mood swings, for instance. Most important, though, for the way in which a woman experiences menopause, is her attitude to it. The ideal would be to view it as potentially a period of intense sexual activity and satisfaction, since the worry of pregnancy, and the inconvenience of periods, will have disappeared.

◆ Does male menopause exist?

Physical and mental symptoms in middle-aged men, identical to those found in menopausal females, suggest to some experts that a male form of this condition exists. The term andropause was accordingly coined (from *andros*, the Greek word for man) in analogical relation to *menos* (month in Greek) to designate the end of male hormonal activity. In reality, no recent scientific research has confirmed this thesis. As we have seen, procreation can continue until an advanced age, and even if there are certain modifications in the hormonal secretions, this does not seem to bring about impotence or a drop in libido. In fact, the passage of time brings about a qualitative difference in the sexual act. Orgasms can become less prolonged and ejaculations slower and weaker. The real sexual aging process is, therefore, psychological. It is believed that retirement, with its associated negative aspects (loss of vitality, giving up sports, no longer working for a living, and, hence, feeling 'useless'), rather than age itself, leads to a reduced or absent sex drive. Becoming a widower can destroy the sexual urge completely. But a shared life, remarriage, or a fling with a younger woman can facilitate a resurgence in sexual energy. Nevertheless, some men do seem to have problems with tiredness, irritability, aching joints, dry skin, insomnia, sweating and hot flushes, and depression in their mid-forties. Male HRT can be given to men with these problems, but its use is still controversial.

◆ *Is it true that failing to have sex regularly reduces the libido?*

An old proverb says that the more you eat, the better your appetite. Put another way, a lack of sexual nourishment, for any reason other than physical debility, can lead to a drop in desire. Abstinence becomes a habit, rather than something exceptional due to fatigue, illness, or loss of partner.

◆ *Does obesity have any effect on sexual behavior?*

Research carried out at the Michael Reese Hospital in Chicago has shown that large women have twice as much sexual desire as thin women, or as those who consume fewer than 1,700 calories per day. It therefore seems probable that plump or fat women have higher hormone levels.

No similar study has been made of the male population; the obese man's sexuality therefore remains a complete mystery.

◆ *At what age is it normal to stop having sexual desires?*

There is no such 'normative' age. Clinical experiments have shown that the real reasons for stopping sex are almost always psychological or cultural.

◆ *What causes sexual impotence?*

There are three types of impotence: primary, secondary, and selective. In the first case, the man can generally get an erection, but never manages to keep it long enough to penetrate his partner. This form of impotence can last for a few months, or even for several years (a few rare cases have been reported in which penetration has never been possible), but it

Can a man become impotent 'overnight'?

The answer is 'Yes,' particularly following damage to the cerebral cortex or spinal column. It can also be caused by a metabolic disorder, such as diabetes, alcohol, or tobacco abuse. Vascular problems can also be at the root of the difficulty.

generally passes after a period of adaptation, particularly if there has not been a change in sexual partner.

Secondary impotence is due to a physical or mental shock that alters the nature of the erection. Finally, selective impotence is associated with a specific partner or sexual context (outside, in the car, at another person's apartment where the couple could be disturbed, etc.) that prevents the individual from achieving full erection. In 50 percent of cases, erectile dysfunction has a physical cause, in which case there is a total absence of erection. This can be due to a congenital anomaly in the sexual organs: malformation of the penis, testicular inadequacy (hypogonadism), or phimosis (an abnormally tight foreskin that makes any attempt at having an erection extremely painful). Some diseases, such as La Peyronie's disease (named for the French physician who discovered it) cause impotence because they involve a hardening of the penis's internal cavities.

Neurological disorders (such as cerebral or spinal lesions) can lead to erectile difficulties, as can endocrinal disturbances or metabolic conditions such as diabetes, alcoholism, or nicotine addiction. Vascular problems also frequently result in impotence. In such cases, either the erection is difficult to achieve and maintain, or the penis remains cold and ejaculation occurs from a limp penis; alternatively the erection is normal but only lasts for up to two minutes. In such cases, the best ways to achieve an erection are in a standing position or lying on one's back.

Finally, certain drugs can cause impotence – for example, some neuroleptics, anti-depressants, tranquilizers, and sleeping pills, but also pain-killers and laxatives. This list is not exhaustive, as particular drugs can interact with each other in such a way as to cause impotence.

The physical reasons for impotence, then, compound underlying mental problems, thus setting up a vicious circle: physical lesion causes impotence which, in turn, leads to psychological problems that only serve to exacerbate the physical disorder. Impotence can also be purely psychological in origin (the sufferer may become over-excited, or over-emotional, or may be prone to depression), such problems gradually causing physical symptoms. The mind–body relationship is thus extremely important in this matter. Deepseated psychological causes of impotence can be found in the way in which the libido developed in early childhood.

◆ My partner has heart disease; is it safe for us to continue having sexual intercourse?

People with heart disease are now encouraged to exercise so long as they recognise their own limitations and stop if they are suffering from angina or obvious signs of cardiac distress. Even after a heart attack, people are encouraged to return to full activity as soon as possible, whereas 20 or 30 years ago, they would have been expected to spend the rest of their lives as a cardiac invalid. Heart disease is very common amongst both men and women from the age of 60 onwards, especially with increasing longevity of life.

Many people are very concerned that sexual activity will increase the likelihood of their partner dying from a heart attack particularly if they already suffer with heart disease. In fact, it is very rare for sudden death to occur during sexual intercourse and when this has happened it has often been accompanied by anxiety, guilt and unfamiliarity with the partner. The strain of lying in bed and wanting to have sex, yet being afraid of the damage it may cause, can be

Can impotence be caused by a psychological problem?

Numerous studies have proved that, in more than one in three cases, psychological problems are the cause of impotence. Impotence is often linked with depression or hyperactive states. Other causes include events in early childhood, or more general social, educational, or religious factors.

more harmful than sexual intercourse itself, especially when this is within a comfortable and familiar relationship. Happy and fulfilling sexual activity with a loving and caring partner can be very therapeutic.

◆ I get very breathless during sexual activity - does this mean that I should stop having a sex life?

Breathlessness may occur for a variety of reasons such as heart or circulation problems, lung disorders, asthma, anaemia or obesity. It may arise suddenly, caused, for example by a chest infection. It is often worse on exertion or at night and should always be reported to a doctor. There is no reason to stop having sexual intercourse, but it may be necessary to use techniques and different positions that will reduce the effort. For example, it may be preferable for the partner who is breathless to be propped up with pillows and it may be more comfortable to make love sitting down.

◆ I suffer from arthritis affecting several joints and I find sexual intercourse very painful. Is there anything I can do to relieve this?

Sex should always be enjoyed, but this may be difficult if every movement causes pain and limbs cannot be moved because of stiffness and rigidity. Arthritis is commoner among people as they get older and particularly affects women; if this affects the hip joint, it may make intercourse difficult if a woman cannot open her legs.

The use of different positions may help to overcome the problem of stiffness and pain and it may also be a good idea to use pillows or cushions to support limbs and stop unnecessary movement.

*W*hat are the major sexually-transmitted diseases?

What precautions should be taken to make love safely?

If you suffer from heart disease, is sex to be avoided?

Here are the guidelines to maintaining a healthy sex life.

◆ **What precautions can be taken against sexually-transmitted diseases?**

Basically, there are three ways of protecting yourself against sexually-transmitted diseases (STDs): by always using a condom, by practicing sexual fidelity, and (the ultimate preventative measure) by abstaining from sex altogether. It is also extremely inadvisable to perform oral sex on a woman during menstruation, as the mouth can contain tiny cuts and abrasions that serve as entry points for sexually-transmitted diseases.

Any exchange of syringes between heroin addicts or other drug users should also be avoided at all costs, as this is one of the main ways in which the hepatitus virus is passed between humans. Hepatitis viruses, it should be remembered, can also be communicated through sexual contact.

◆ **What are the major sexually-transmitted diseases?**

Gonorrhea
Gonorrhea is caused by a germ, *neisseria gonorrhoeae*. Symptoms manifest themselves from one to five days after infection. In men, it causes a frequent desire to urinate and a burning sensation during urination. In most cases, the urethra excretes a clear, purulent liquid. If gonorrhea is not treated, or is treated

Are STDs only caught through sexual contact?

Unfortunately, no. Certain STDs can be passed on by mouth contact, through a cut in the skin, or by means of syringes, infected water, or inadequate sanitary hygiene.

too late, it can affect the prostate or the seminal vesicles and cause sterility.

In women, the symptoms of gonorrhea are often difficult to detect: they include a frequent desire to urinate, a slight burning sensation during urination, and a thick white discharge. As the latter type of discharge is also common in healthy women, victims of the disease often delay in seeking treatment. But once again, if gonorrhea is left untreated, or is treated too late, it can result in sterility as the fallopian tubes become blocked, thereby preventing the sperm from reaching the ovum.

In both sexes, gonorrhea can affect other parts of the body: additional symptoms include weeping erosions of the anal mucous membranes; nose and throat infections caused by oral sex; infections that can result in articular or cutaneous complications combined with pustules forming, generally on the external sexual organs (the labia majora or the shaft of the penis).

Healthy gonorrhea carriers exist among both sexes, but particularly among women, who can transmit the disease without suffering from any of its symptoms.

Herpes

Six days after contact with an infected person the sufferer will feel pain, tenderness and an itchy sensation near the penis or vagina. Single or multiple blisters soon appear in the penis or on the vulva.

Trichomonas and chlamydiae

Trichomonas are organisms that cause Trichomonas vaginitis, a vaginal infection characterized by a greenish, often putrid discharge. This organism is transmitted sexually, but also by water, soiled objects and by toiletry items.

Chlamydiae are tiny bacteria, about the size of a virus, which develop, like viruses, inside the

What does the frequent urge to urinate indicate?

This, together with other apparently trivial symptoms – an unusual white discharge, general aches and pains, and even a pain behind the eyes – should not be ignored. They could be signs of a more serious problem.

chlamydiae cells they have infected. Infection with chlamydiae trachomatis is the most common sexually-transmitted disease in the western world. In women, they are responsible for over one-third of the cases of salpingitis, an infection of the fallopian tubes that can lead to sterility. In men, *chlamydiae* are responsible for forms of urethritis that are generally less severe than those caused by gonorrhea, but they can sometimes result in serious complications: epididymitis (infection of the epididymis, which is part of the system of sperm ducts), prostatitis, or articular ailments. In both sexes, *chlamydiae* are also responsible for infections of the lungs or eyes, such as trachoma, a chronic contagious conjunctivitis.

In many cases, *trichomonas* and *chlamydiae* are found together in genital infections.

Syphilis

The discovery of antibiotics in the 1940s has greatly reduced the importance of this disease, once nicknamed 'the pox,' which ravaged humankind for hundreds of years.

It is estimated that the disease has made a comeback since the appearance of AIDS in the 1980s, and since the social changes of the 1960s. Syphilis is caused by a bacterium, known as *pale treponema*, and there are three phases of development.

The average incubation phase lasts for three weeks and is characterized by the appearance of a small circular sore, which is soft to the touch, sometimes has secretions and is situated on the genitalia, anus or tonsils. This is referred to as the soft chancre. After about five to ten days, the rim of the chancre hardens, becoming red and glossy.

This is accompanied by a lymphatic attack in the infected area. The chancre is painless and, if left untreated, will heal and disappear of its own accord after three to five weeks. But the

disease continues its evolution. Sometimes several chancres appear.

The secondary phase occurs about 45 days after the appearance of the first chancre, or chancres. This is the most contagious period, as the disease is practically invisible, but the infection is becoming generalized. This continues during a three- to four-year period and is marked by the following symptoms:

• Appearance of the syphilitic roseola, a skin eruption consisting of pale pink rashes that do not cause itching and are generally found on the belly, flanks and back. These rashes disappear after one or two months.

• Appearance of painless ulcers on the mucous membranes, particularly those of the mouth and genitals.

• Appearance of ganglions, generally on the posterior cervical area, or on the elbows.

The third phase occurs after three to four years and is characterized by deep cutaneous lesions that gradually replace more superficial ones. This phase can result in serious attacks on the cardiovascular system, particularly the aorta, and on the nervous system, with a risk of syphilitic meningitis and/or tabes, and degenerative lesions of the nerves that can notably cause coordination difficulties.

Syphilis is transmitted by sexual contact – intercourse, petting, or oral sex (which leads to infection of the tonsils) – but also by soiled objects such as glasses, towels, or toiletry items.

Viral hepatitis

These infections are characterized by necrosis (tissue death) and by inflammation of the liver. Some types can be sexually transmitted. Hepatitis A can be transmitted orally. Kissing is therefore a common means of transmission, through virus-infected saliva. Hepatitis B is transmitted by sexual contact or infected blood; it often occurs in drug addicts. Both kinds of

Has syphilis been eradicated?

While the number of cases has declined dramatically due to the discovery of antibiotics, it is now thought that the disease could be making a comeback.

hepatitis result in asthenia (profound fatigue), anorexia, and light fever. Icterus, or jaundice, as it is more often called, is a common feature of all types of hepatitis. Symptoms develop after an incubation period of one to six months, during which time it remains contagious. It can last longer, however, either through a series of relapses or from one single outbreak. Hepatitis B is more serious than hepatitis A and has a mortality rate of 5–20 percent. Hepatitis C is very similar in form to Hepatitis B.

Aids

AIDS, or Acquired Immune Deficiency Syndrome, covers a large number of symptoms that occur in patients whose natural defense mechanisms no longer function normally. When confronted by a germ, parasite or virus, the body produces antibodies to attack the disease. HIV, the AIDS virus, causes a sort of paralysis of this immune defense system.

It is for this reason that the disorders that AIDS patients can suffer from are so varied. Typically, these include fungal infections, especially those caused by *Candida albicans*, which can produce various symptoms: intertrigo (a bright red, sometimes weeping infection of the skin folds, for example, in the groin area), stomatitis (total infection of the mouth's mucous membranes), genital infections, and septicemia (a multiplication of bacteria in the blood). Ulcers may also appear on the mouth, the mucous membranes and the genitalia. In addition there can be episodes of herpes.

Apart from septicemia, all of these illnesses are benign when antibodies are able to perform their normal defensive role; they become dangerous when the body is no longer able to defend itself. The course of AIDS is often complicated by *Pneumocystis carinii* pneumonia (a rare lung disease) or Kaposi's sarcoma (an unusual form of cancer).

The most common early warning signs of AIDS are weight loss and fever, with no obvious cause, followed by persistent diarrhea and fungal infections, often caused by *Candida albicans*. Thrush coats the tongue with white spots. Adenopathies (swelling of the lymph nodes) develop, as well as cutaneous eruptions on the face that cause desquamation, a peeling away of the skin.

A heavy chest cough and general itching also develop. Finally, many patients sweat abundantly at night. However, with the exception of *Pneumocystis carinii* pneumonia and Kaposi's sarcoma, none of these signs proves the presence of AIDS.

We now know the disease's favorite targets: the lungs, the digestive tract, the skin, and the brain. The disease is transmitted sexually and through blood. Other possible means of communication, notably oral sex, have not been satisfactorily proven. However, it is not advisable to perform oral sex on a woman during menstruation.

Before the disease manifests itself, there is an initial period during which the person is HIV-positive, but there are no visible symptoms.

Sexually-transmitted diseases can be prevented by using condoms and by practicing sexual fidelity – clearly both partners have to agree to respect this commitment for it to be effective. The case of viral hepatitis is more complex, as it can be transmitted by saliva.

◆ What is safe sex?

Safe sex includes all the possible ways of preventing contamination from STDs. Primarily it refers to mechanical means such as the condom or the thin latex strips that are used to prevent transmission during the performance of fellatio. The expression is also used to designate the various sexual acts that do not involve penetration: oral and manual sex, and varied foreplay. Practicing safe sex is an individual, as well as collective, part of our contemporary way of life. Woody Allen famously remarked that masturbation, that most extreme version of safe sex, involves having sex with the person you love most. Americans are active proponents of safe sex, organizing 'circle jerk' parties, where people of both sexes participate in nonpenetrative caresses.

◆ Is making love dangerous for coronary patients?

Making love does not have to involve highly energetic athletics. In fact, it should be no more dangerous than having a medical check-up. But intercourse is notably less stressful when performed in a familiar, loving context such as marriage, or a long-lasting affair. Adulterous relations can lead to feelings of guilt, giving a far stronger emotional charge. The moral of this is that coronary patients should remain sexually faithful to their partners.

◆ Is anal sex harmful?

Anal intercourse takes place when the penis is inserted through the anus into the rectum of the partner. Some people find anal intercourse very stimulating and exciting, because the anus has a lot of nerve endings. It can be very stimulating for both men and women, although women will not get an orgasm from anal intercourse alone. While some heterosexual couples try it occasionally, it is more common amongst homosexual men. Because the anus itself is quite small, both men and women can

What are the first symptoms of AIDS?

A loss of weight accompanied by fever, both with no apparent cause, is the first indication. This is followed by severe diarrhea and a yeast infection – similar to thrush – on the mouth and tongue, which becomes covered with white spots.

find penetration painful and the use of a lubricant is often helpful. It is very important to ensure that the lubricant is a water-based one, as oil-based lubricants can damage the condom. Pregnancy cannot result from purely anal intercourse, but it is important to use a condom because of the risk of sexually-transmitted diseases. The anal sphincter and surrounding tissue can easily be damaged during anal sex as the tissue is thin and the anus not designed for heavy thrusting. The risk of transmission of sexual diseases is particularly high with anal intercourse, especially if the anus is torn, and AIDS researchers believe that anal intercourse is the single most important factor in the spread of the HIV virus.

In order to perform anal sex safely, it is important to adhere to these guidelines:
1. Always wash the penis thoroughly both before and after anal sex, as the anus and rectum are full of bacteria.
2. Always use a condom with a water-based not oil-based lubricant.
3. Never insert the penis into the vagina after anal sex without first removing the condom and washing the penis.

◆ What does oral sex involve?

Oral sex was represented in the *Kama Sutra* and seems to have been much more acceptable in the past than in the present day. It was viewed as essentially part of foreplay, before penetration took place leading to ejaculation and orgasm. But oral sex can conclude with orgasm without moving on to penetration. Obviously, oral sex without penetration will not carry with it a risk of pregnancy, as the sperm have not entered the vagina.

Oral sex refers to mouth-to-genital contact; if a woman's clitoris or labia are stimulated by a partner's tongue or mouth, then it is called cunnilingus. If the stimulation is to the man's penis, then it is called fellatio. Oral sex may involve either heterosexual or homosexual relationships and if both partners stimulate each other simultaneously, then it is known as the '69' position.

Fellatio is also known by the slang expressions a 'blow-job' and 'giving head.' Fellatio does not involve blowing, and some women have inadvertently injured their partners because they have not realized this.

Most people use their mouth and tongue to kiss and lick their partners, not only in the genital area, but also around the body. The term for this is 'going around the world.'

◆ Can medical drugs affect sexual performance?

The short answer to this question is, yes, many drugs given for the treatment of medical conditions can affect sexual performance and desire. In men, some drugs may affect libido, erection, and/or ejaculation; in women, libido and orgasmic ability may be impaired.

Tranquilizers, sedatives, and antidepressant drugs have all been shown to inhibit sexual drive, impair libido, and slow arousal in both men and women. Medicines used for the treatment of high blood pressure can also affect sexual function adversely; they can affect arousal and desire, but may also cause inhibition or failure of erection and ejaculation in men. Water tablets, or diuretics, can trigger erectile failure, and men on these drugs are twice as likely to be impotent as those not on drugs. Androgens, or the male hormones, have been considered to increase sexual desire in both men and women; men with low levels of these hormones may have a depressed sexual appetite. Estrogens do not seem to affect libido in either women or men.

Index